The Greatest Gene

One Airman's Life

December 2015

To Jim and Mary,
Thought you might like to meet
"Uncle Mike".
Hope you enjoy the story.
Cheers, Dick

by

Richard C Henneberry

ISBN:978-0692378137
ISBN-13:0692378138

The DayDreamer Press

Viera, Florida

Published in the United States of America

Dedicated to

S/Sgt Michael R Henneberry (1920-1989)

The Men of the VIII Bomber Command/8th Air Force

The Women Airforce Service Pilots (WASP)

And All the Members of the Greatest Generation
who answered their country's call

Cover photograph by Richard F Henneberry II

Uncle Mike, circa 1985

Acknowledgements

I would like to express my gratitude to the US Air Force Historical Studies Office (AF/HOH) at Bolling AFB; the response to my request for information exceeded all expectations and bolstered my confidence that I could tell this story accurately. It is fitting that our government continues to support all efforts of those who wish to honor our veterans and to keep their memories alive; it should be considered part of the contract with those who served.

The National Museum of the Mighty 8th Air Force, just off I-95 in Pooler, Georgia, was also a major source of information about operations in the air campaign against Germany in WW II. Thanks are due its many volunteers and supporters who have made it a major force in preserving the history of aviation during this critical time. Thanks are also definitely due to the authors of the many web sites displaying great quantities of information about all aspects of US efforts in WWII. They are too numerous to mention but I have listed several important internet sources, along with several books by survivors, in the "Further Reading" section at the end of the book. I have perused many such writings and been informed by them all while making every effort to avoid plagiarizing any of them.

The entire Henneberry family owes its gratitude to my son, Michael Patrick Henneberry, for "finding" Uncle Mike and reintroducing him to us. As Yogi Berra might have said, he made this story necessary.

I am indebted to the friends and relatives who carefully read this book, especially Kathleen Younger and Martha Mower. They offered numerous corrections and constructive suggestions; any errors remaining are my fault. Thanks also go to Andrew Corrow for photos of his father, Henry Corrow, and to Ken Younger for information about his father, KG Younger, Jr. Finally, I must accord my wife, Pat, special accolades for listening to the endless war stories as I became immersed in the details of this book and for repeated readings of the manuscript.

CONTENTS

Other Books by this Author

A Daydreamer's Digest
Tales from the Berkshires
by Richard C Henneberry
ISBN: 978-0615700137
Daydreamer Press
Viera, Florida 2012

Remembering Flo
by Richard C Henneberry
ISBN-13: 978-0692375112
Daydreamer Press
Viera, Florida 2015

Preface

This is a true story. My son's discovery of my father's long-lost brother was an incredible coincidence but that is the way it happened. What I have written in Part I about this improbable event is based on the way it was told to me independently by the two people involved. One definition of "miraculous" is "improbable and extraordinary and bringing very welcome consequences". The adjective seems made to order for the story.

Part II is written from SSgt Michael R Henneberry's point of view posthumously with me as his ghost writer. It describes his life in the Army and is based on my own first-hand knowledge of the people and events involved supplemented by extensive research at US Military archives and at both military and civilian history sites on the internet as well as books written by survivors of the war (see Further Reading). Extensive documentation of the 14 October 1943 mission of Lucifer II – the Second Schweinfurt raid on "Black Thursday" - and the fate of its crew was provided by the USAF Historical Studies Office. A lifelong interest in aviation, my experience as a USAF Officer, and my years as a general aviation pilot provided me with some insights into the military and aviation aspects of the story. Finally, Uncle Mike's extended visits with us at our home in Maryland in his later years gave me the opportunity to learn some details of his life directly from him. Parts I and III are factual descriptions of events in my own voice as narrator. I have attempted to keep this story as close to the facts as possible but for the sake of continuity it was sometimes necessary in Part II to fill in the blanks with my best estimate of what may have happened. I describe this part of the book as historical fiction.

Regrettably, several of the photos did not reproduce well but that was the best we could do with the old prints from as long ago as 1918. Also, some readers may find the organization of the book somewhat confusing as we go from the 1980s in Part I to the 1940s in Part II and back to the 1980s in Part III with two different voices telling the story. That's just the way I thought it came together best.

So here is the saga of my Uncle Mike, told here not as a chapter from history but as the story of an Airman's life. It is the story of a man who made his contributions as a member of the Greatest Generation and it suggests that there are other ways, short of dying, in which people give their lives for their country.

RCH, 4 July 2015

*"Older men declare war.
But it is the youth that
must fight and die."*

Herbert Hoover

Part I

Miraculous Encounter

Chapter 1

Pearl Harbor, 1982

During Christmas vacation of his senior year at Villanova University, our son Michael decided to exercise one of the few "perks" available to Naval ROTC cadets: space-available travel on military aircraft. "Space-A" is easy on the pocketbook but can try the patience of a saint; for every hour spent in the air, many more are spent waiting in military terminals for the next available seat heading in the right general direction. But Mike had almost three weeks free and what might generously be called a modest budget, so this was his best bet for a vacation beyond the borders of his home state. Donning his "Winter Blues" and meeting up with a couple of fellow Villanova cadets in Philadelphia, off they went: target Hawaii and the sands of Waikiki!

Our fledgling sailors' luck held as far as Naval Air Station Alameda in Oakland Bay where they were surprised to learn that Space-A Travel eligibility for people in their cadet status only extended to the contiguous 48 states; they were not eligible for a "hop" to Hawaii. Demonstrating the kind of initiative the Navy likes to see in its officers, Mike's reaction was to look for a creative way around the regulations. His traveling companions were getting a bit nervous however, and opted to turn around and head for home. Mike, feeling an unidentified force drawing him to Hawaii, decided to play out his cards and see what turned up. He is usually a guy who likes to have his friends around and it seems a bit out of character for him to travel alone but, he later explained, Hawaii - which he had never visited before - was drawing him like a magnet. Pushing his luck a bit further, our intrepid mariner talked his way into the Alameda Officers Club, normally off-limits to NROTC cadets. Fortunately, the part-timer checking ID cards was no whiz when it came to rules and regulations so Mike headed for the bar figuring the bartender wouldn't know one set of epaulets from another and the customers had other things on their minds. After a couple of beers, he struck up a conversation with a young Navy Pilot and soon found himself in a discussion destined to alter the lives of a host of Henneberrys. By some strange twist of luck, Mike's new drinking buddy was having an early night at the O-Club in honor of the fact that he would be flying a P-3 to Naval Air Station Pearl Harbor at 0500. Since he was within his personal "8 hours from bottle to throttle" rule, he had switched to seltzer and was ready to call it a night. But, drunk or sober, he wasn't at all interested in any restrictions on the passengers he could stick in his empty seats; Mike was in a US Navy uniform and that was good enough for him. "The seat's yours if you want it buddy, but one thing – bring a warm blanket. It gets mighty damned cold in that back seat".

And so Michael Patrick Henneberry arrived in Pearl Harbor where his luck served him once more as he latched onto a room in the Navy's transient quarters, a short walk from some of the world's greatest beaches. Soon, long days of Hawaiian hospitality and sunshine consumed not only all his energy but all his funds as well, and soon I received a telegram from my son asking "Could you please send me $75?" I did, but this brought our traveler to the realization that even the best of times must end. It was time to pack up and start planning for the inevitable trip home, and it was soon necessary to check in at the Naval Air Station for a flight back to the States.

Since departures from military air terminals usually begin near dawn, the wee small hours are best for signing up for an empty seat so by 0300 Mike was in line. But he knew that this time he wouldn't be dealing with a friendly P-3 pilot in the Officer's Club, but with a sailor behind the counter who knew the rules of Space-A travel inside-and-out and was well aware of the fact that he was authorized to enforce them. And he looked like he had been in the Navy long enough to know an ROTC Cadet's uniform when he saw one. Mike wasn't sure how all this would work out but he wasn't looking forward to the idea of calling his father asking for the price of an airline ticket home, so at this point there was nothing left to do but to walk confidently to the counter just like he knew what he was doing. Mike gave his name to the clerk and that's when the fun began. "Don't pull my leg at this hour – I just signed you in a minute ago" the sailor announced. Mike pointed to his Navy name tag and tried again, only to get a slightly saltier version of the first reply.

After a minute or two of this - increasing in volume with each exchange - an older gentleman stepped up to the counter and joined the fray, demanding to know why his name was being bandied about. But there was no mistake, they both had the same unusual name. Strangely enough, two Michael Henneberrys - completely unknown to each other – met at the Space-A counter at Pearl Harbor in the middle of a January night in 1983. Ours is not a common name, and two bearers of the name bumping into each other in such unlikely circumstances suggested that certain questions might be asked, and so they were.

"Young Mike"had no idea who this fellow was who shared his name, but he had a feeling that this unlikely meeting must mean something special. The older gent turned out to be a retired Army Air Forces / US Air Force veteran and POW. Using his own Space-A perk, he was off on an ambitious month-long trip to Australia and New Zealand. At first "Old Mike" was thoroughly confused, but he had a few questions: "Is your father's name Richard?" and "Was your father born in Yonkers?" When Young Mike answered yes to both questions, the old fellow felt a sudden need to sit down. Yet something didn't make sense – until suddenly he understood: he had skipped a generation - it wasn't his brother's son he was talking to, it was his brother's grandson! The improbability of this coincidence was compounded by the fact that "Old Mike" had not been in touch with any of his relatives for 25 years; he was not yet aware of the fact that his brother Richard - my father - had been dead almost 20 years. In fact, he didn't know it, but he was the last survivor of the seven Henneberry siblings from Yonkers. Yet here in the middle of the night, in Hawaii where no Henneberry of ours had ever before traveled, sat two Michael Henneberrys, closely related strangers who had met by a strange quirk of fate.

While "Old Mike" - known to us all as Uncle Mike from then on - resumed his adventure to Australia, our son Mike continued on the homeward leg of his trip and called us a few days later from Kansas where he waited for the next Space-A ride heading east. The dispatch clerk at Pearl, after some convincing by the old Sergeant, had finally agreed to put our son on the next flight for the States "Just to get rid of him". Mike said everything was fine and he was just calling to let us know he was safe and sound and on his way home, but I soon realized he had really called because he wanted to relate the strange story of his improbable encounter. As he began to tell me the story I had a strong premonition of what he was about to say. For whatever reason, the thought had persisted in my mind over the previous 25 years that Uncle Mike would turn up again. As strange as it seems, I was not truly surprised when my son told me he had.

Chapter 2

Yonkers, 1958

I had no trouble remembering the last time I had seen my Uncle Mike; it was the night of his mother's – my grandmother's - wake in Yonkers in November, 1958. It was his first trip back to his home town in about a dozen years and I guess he felt he had received a cool reception from his family - again. I suppose he was still the rebellious loner with the chip on his shoulder I had come to understand he was, and he didn't stick around long at the funeral home; in fact he left before I arrived with my parents. I was a senior in college at the time, and we received the news of my grandmother's death on the day I arrived home for what I expected would be my last home-cooked Thanksgiving Dinner for a long time. In a few months I would become the property of the US Air Force and be off, so I traveled with my parents from our home in Western Massachusetts for my dad's mother's funeral in my old home town of Yonkers.

I had learned that Uncle Mike had returned to Yonkers for his mother's funeral and I hoped I would get to see him. I was an eight year-old kid when I last saw him at a family gathering shortly after he came home from the war; enough time had passed for him to notice some changes in the kid he met then. It it easy to say now that I had felt a premonition that our destinies were somehow linked, but how can I be sure of what I felt so many years ago? Although we were born just seventeen years apart, we were of different generations. I was a young boy when he went off to war, and I clearly remember his visit to us in Maine in 1943 while he was en route to his new base in England. I also have a clear memory of the clipping from the Yonkers *Herald Statesman* reporting him missing in action over Germany; I saved that clipping until two years later when my grandparents got the telegram from the Red Cross telling them that their son had turned up alive, if somewhat the worse for wear, in a liberated POW camp in Austria. The telegram reporting him alive was a complete surprise; after Uncle Mike was reported missing in October of 1943, nothing more had been heard about him until the Red Cross telegram.

The Geneva Convention requires captors to register prisoners of war with the International Red Cross as part of the agency's role in monitoring prison camps. It turned out that my Uncle was not the first prisoner Nazi Germany failed to register. As is well known now, that was not the only provision of the Convention they refused to abide by, even though Germany, unlike Japan, was a signatory to the Convention of 1929. So everyone at home had given Uncle Mike up for dead, thus there were no letters for him coming from home. Nor did any of the letters he remembered sending ever reach home, not surprising since the Red Cross mediated the exchange of messages between POWs and the outside world. And, of course, since the Red Cross had not been advised of his status as a prisoner he did not receive any of the relief packages the Germans finally began permitting the agency to send in November 1943.

Back to the night of my grandmother's wake. From comments I had overheard in the family, I had been led to believe that Uncle Mike was what was called a "drinking man" in those days. It didn't take a college education to decide where to start looking for him after he slipped away from the funeral home. I got as far as the first bar on South Broadway. This was our first ever meeting with both of us as adults. For the first time I was a lot bigger than he was and for the first time I slid up on a bar stool beside him and ordered a beer. I was hoping to hear a little about his experiences in the Air Force, especially his time as a prisoner of war, but he never mentioned it so I didn't either.

I don't remember what we talked about and I'm sure he didn't tell me much about his post-war travels except to mention California. He asked me a little about myself and where I was heading in life. I know he was pleased to hear I would be graduating from college the following spring – the first of our Henneberry clan to do so - and I could see he was especially pleased to hear I would receive an Air Force Commission at graduation and would be entering pilot training shortly thereafter. At some point while writing this narrative I suddenly realized that Uncle Mike, although he would never say so, was proud of his military experience and his survival adventures during and after the War, including nearly two years as a guest of the Third Reich. He was still a soldier deep down inside and maybe he felt some camaraderie with others who wore the uniform. Whatever tenuous bond might have existed between us before that evening seemed to grow a little stronger in that short hour in a bar in Yonkers the night before my grandmother was laid to rest. This is a bond that many Americans today, most of whom have never served in the military, don't seem to understand. Only 20% of the members of the current congress, and only about 8% of the total US population have had any military experience. To them, those in the military are just the people they hire to fight their wars – which may help explain why we enter into so many wars.

Shortly after his mother's funeral, Uncle Mike, remembering his dislike for the cold New York winters and resenting all over again the cold shoulder he always seemed to get from his relatives, headed off once more for the West Coast. He overlooked the small detail of telling anyone in the family where he was going and as the years passed he never quite got around to letting anyone know where he was. But now, in Pearl Harbor in 1983 - 25 years after my uncle and I had a couple of beers in that bar on South Broadway - the family connections he had ignored or avoided for so long were reestablished. When our son Mike invited his newly discovered Uncle to his college graduation and Navy Commissioning the following spring in Pennsylvania, Uncle Mike came back east for a visit. He was visibly pleased to see Mike receive his Navy Commission. Before his visit, when he learned that our old friend and neighbor of more than twenty years, Len Taylor, planned to present our son Mike with Len's own ceremonial sword from his days as a Naval Officer, Uncle Mike arranged to have the sword suitably engraved with our son's name and commissioning date as his graduation gift. He killed several birds with one stone on his first trip; our daughter Kathy – the Irish twin of our son Michael – also graduated from Villanova the same day as her brother and that was enough to kick off a couple of big parties, so Uncle Mike got to meet lots of friends and relations.

Mom pins on Mike's gold bars

Uncle Mike came back East again when our daughter Ellen graduated from college two years later, and again two years after that just for the sake of a visit. Each trip he came to our home and stayed three or four weeks and so we were able to spend a lot of time together. It was during those visits that I was able to fill in some of the blanks from what I call Uncle Mike's "eclipse" years, but it was very difficult to pin him down with the fine details. Not that he was trying to hide anything - he just wasn't good at getting the details out. And, like so many others, he had no desire to talk about his days as a POW. After being liberated, debriefed, and shipped back to the States late in 1945, he was discharged from the Army Air Forces and it was then that he returned home to what he thought was a lukewarm welcome.

Thinking the Army felt more like home to him than Yonkers did, he reenlisted in June 1946, getting his Staff Sargent rank back. Stationed in the Pacific Northwest, he met and married Lillian and had a son named Ward.

Ward Henneberry visited with us for a weekend when he was in Washington DC on business in the late 1980s, and I enjoyed his company. He had served with the Green Berets in Viet Nam and now works in something to do with computer applications in the banking industry in Seattle. Several strange coincidences are reported in this book, and Ward and I share another one: if one had searched the Amazon website in 2013 for the name Henneberry one would have found quite a few books by authors with that name, but finding Ward's book and mine listed one after the other in the Amazon catalog was more than a little surprising. It seems he co-authored a banking-related book on computer programming in the C# language. We call such things coincidences but aren't they really inevitabilities when authors' names are catalogued alphabetically? The coincidence was that we both authored books. In any event, I didn't learn too much about his dad from Ward when he visited us. They went decades without seeing each other after the marriage broke up but did get together several times later in life. By then Ward had a young daughter, Megan, born in 1978. I think Uncle Mike had never really had the chance to spend much time with young people but it was obvious from what he told me that he was smitten by his granddaughter in the limited time they spent together. Ward did tell me that after Mike and Lillian were married they moved in with Lillian's Mother and Ward had heard stories that there was friction between the trio. Whatever factors were involved, the marriage was short-lived and Uncle Mike was off again.

About a year later S/Sgt Michael Henneberry was transferred from the Army Air Forces into the US Air Force on the day it was created, 18 September 1947. He kept his rank of staff sergeant but now the abbreviation didn't include the slash; the new Air Force simplified it to SSgt. This was, of course, the same USAF I was commissioned in twelve years later, but Uncle Mike wasn't around to render the traditional first salute to the brand new Second Lieutenant; a stranger got my $1.00. By the time I came on board, his failing health had long since forced him to accept a disability retirement. His pancreas had ceased functioning by 1948, he had a lung removed at Fitzsimmons Army Hospital in the early 1950s, and he suffered from a significant case of what would now be called chronic obstructive pulmonary disease (COPD) - problems traceable directly to his POW days and the malnutrition, the cold, and the diseases most POWs experienced, especially near the end of the war. Despite his wartime experience he showed no signs of post-traumatic stress disorder but his health issues prevented him from staying in an assignment long enough to be considered for promotion. He retired on disability as a Staff Sergeant about 18 years after he enlisted in 1937.

Although Uncle Mike never expressed it, it was clear that his visits to us in later years were important to him. I felt I knew what he wanted from us: he needed to know who we Henneberrys were – including himself. He realized his time was winding down and he was searching for his roots. Old Mike wanted one other thing from us, I think. His visits were the nearest he had come to living in the heart of a family with dogs and young people and not too many dull moments. He was not a man who wore his heart on his sleeve but I think he realized he had missed something in life and there were few second chances - maybe he considered this a second chance and he wasn't about to pass it up.

And so, during these visits and in the letters we exchanged, I was able to start putting together the story of this old soldier's life - not an especially happy story - but a story with so many unlikely twists that it seems to me worth telling. In one sense it is a commentary on the price extracted from those who return from the wars their elders - who stay at home - send them off to fight.

Six smiling faces: Kathy (l), Ellen, Uncle Mike, Rich, Kieran (l) and Shandy

Uncle Mike and his favorite" bookends"
at our home in Maryland, circa 1984

Chapter 3

The Henneberrys

I have misty memories of Uncle Mike's occasional visits during my early years in Yonkers, but my first clear recollection of him goes back to 1942. I am sure of the year because my Father's government position had taken us to Bangor, Maine that first summer of US involvement in World War II. Uncle Mike spent a few days with us before shipping out from Dow Army Air Field bound for England and his gunner's duties on a B-17. To a 5 year old boy it was a big deal to have a soldier visiting, and his own Uncle at that.

So who are these Henneberrys? Just regular people, nothing special, but maybe with a story worth telling. Michael Raymond was the last of seven children born to Richard Steven Henneberry and Mary Sharky Henneberry between 1909 and 1920. Uncle Mike's father, who I always called "Pop" (I suppose because that was what my father called him) had been born on the family farm in Ardmore, County Waterford, Ireland in 1887. When his father (another Richard Henneberry) died, Pop and his brother Michael (yes, another Michael Henneberry), realizing the farm would go to their eldest brother as dictated by British law at the time (the Brits always did what they could to increase emigration from Ireland), decided to head for Wales to join an uncle mining coal. Their plan was to save enough for their passage to America with its streets paved with gold and then to go on to make their fortunes.

By the end of 1905, my grandfather and his brother had returned to Ireland with the price of transatlantic passage in their pockets and soon set off across the westward ocean. They departed from the port in Cobh, Ireland – the same port from which my mother would depart some 22 years later. No coincidence there; most of the millions who left Ireland early in the Twentieth Century departed from Cobh, known as Queenstown from 1850 until the 1920s - for reasons you can probably guess. Pop's crossing on *The Cedric* took eight days and on 23 February 1906 my grandfather arrived at Ellis Island with $10 in his pocket and, with his brother Michael, joined another brother, Martin, in Yonkers.

Pop's brother and travel companion Michael came a lot closer to making his fortune than Pop did. This Uncle Mike was a clever fellow who held several patents later in his career at the Alexander Smith Rug Factory – well known in Yonkers as the "Carpet Shop". I still have a clear memory of his pleasant, single family home in a nice section of the city. I remember his wife, Aunt Jessie, and her wonderful, soft Scottish burr and I have isolated memories of their children. Strangely enough, I still have a letter written to Uncle Mike – the subject of our story – from one of these children, Billy, in the 1960s. They had known each other as youngsters and both had spent careers in military service, something they were proud of. Maybe it was no coincidence that Uncle Mike gravitated toward my son and myself who had also worn the uniform proudly. Maybe he had a lot of time to think of concepts like patriotism and loyalty during his days in the POW camp and maybe he felt a stronger affinity toward those who had also served.

My grandfather, Pop, did okay too, though he never became as prosperous as his brother. Pop worked his whole adult life in the Otis Elevator shop in Yonkers as a machinist, a skill he had acquired on-the-job. I think he was proud of the fact that he held his job and raised a large family through the depths of the Great Depression, an accomplishment in those days. But he never achieved the dream I am certain he had since leaving the family farm in Ardmore; he never got that little plot of ground to call his own.

Pop was a quiet man without much to say. Even when I was a kid I could tell he missed the life on the small farm he left behind in Ireland in exchange for a nondescript apartment in the new world. His gift to me was the love of growing vegetables and flowers. When I would arrive for my annual springtime visit Pop would lead me directly to the little tomato plants growing in containers on his windowsill. He would send me home with most of those plants and a few vegetable seeds and careful directions for their planting and care. For years as an adult I had large vegetable gardens – as much as 3,000 square feet during our Maryland years. They were gardens to be proud of and even now, more than sixty-five years after Pop got me started, I never let a summer go by without the raised beds near my back door overflowing with tomato and pepper plants and a few other fresh delectables mixed in with marigolds and morning glories.

Pop married Mary Sharky, my grandmother, in 1907. I know nothing of her origins beyond the fact that she was born in White Plains of parents who had both immigrated from Ireland. She was a pleasant, soft-spoken woman who always had time for me despite her being surrounded by a large family and seeming always busy. The thing I remember most about her is that she always encouraged me to do something with myself. When I was about 12 or 13 years old she decided I had a promising singing voice and, since nobody else was doing anything about it, she took me off to a voice teacher. I had a clear tenor voice in those days and I knew all the words to all the Tin Pan Alley songs about

Ireland after countless hours of listening to the likes of Bing Crosby, Lanny Ross, and Dennis Day on the radio and I would belt out the tunes at a moment's notice. But my singing career was very short-lived; Grandma had failed to allow for the effects of the male hormones that began wreaking havoc on my vocal cords about the time of my first lesson. But thanks to Grandma, for years in my youth I was a fan of Jack Sharkey, the former heavyweight boxing champion, thinking we must be distant cousins – only years later did I learn that Jack's real name was Joseph Paul Zukauskas.

The first child born to Grandma and Pop was Richard, my father, then Mary, always called May to distinguish her from her mother. She was followed by John, then Katherine, always known to me as Aunt Kaye. Then Joe, Vinnie, and finally Michael Raymond - the seven of them spread over eleven years. From my childhood, I remember a big family getting together often for impromptu parties. My guess is that this is the kind of family Uncle Mike – the subject of our story - left behind when he became a soldier in 1937. But as I grew up I learned that, like all families, some unhappy times had come along. In fact, in retrospect it seems that my father and his siblings had more than their share of bad luck. One of them had a child institutionalized for many years with what I believe to have been a bipolar disorder. Another had a Down's Syndrome child.

The report that Mike was missing in action and presumed dead was tragedy enough for the year 1943 but that same year my dad's sister Kaye, everybody's favorite person, lost her leg, her health, and ultimately her life in a Manhattan Subway accident; caught in the press of the crowd to get aboard she slipped under the wheels of a departing train. Aunt Kaye was truly a person everyone loved. She had a brilliant, ever-present smile and a lovely, clear singing voice. I remember her as the kind of person who would light up a room just by entering it. After her accident her health began a steady decline due to an amputation site that wouldn't heal sufficiently to accept a prosthesis. She was confined to a hospital or nursing home for the rest of her life and eventually contracted tuberculosis. But her spirit was undaunted through it all. I remember visiting her in Grasslands Hospital in Valhalla in 1951, about 8 years after her accident. She was getting around in a wheelchair by then but her smile was as bright as ever and her singing was heard every day in every ward on her floor – she had made it her job to cheer up the patients as she carried her zither and her songs from room to room. It would be the last time I would see her alive.

Sadly, Aunt Kaye became another example – like her brother Michael Raymond – of a person whose life is stolen away by a sequence of events beyond his or her control. The bad luck continued, though not until a dozen years later, with my father's sudden death in an accident at age 56. But well before that, the family Uncle Mike came home to in 1945 was not the one he left behind in 1937 when he put on the uniform of the US Army.

Part II

Uncle Mike's Story

Chapter 4

Army Life

As I watched the rocky coast of Maine slip behind us, I thought about my visit with my brother Richie and his family in Orono. Although he was my oldest brother and eleven years my senior, he was the only one in my family I could have a decent conversation with without all that "Raymond you should do this, Raymond you should do that" stuff. Richie was still living at home until I was nearly 15, and I think he took me on as a "project". When I was getting in a lot of fights at school he asked me if I thought I had a talent for fighting and whisked me off to the gym at the YMCA. It seemed like fun for a while, taking my frustrations out on a bag and all, but then in my first Golden Gloves fight I learned that some of those little guys can really hit back – so my first fight was also my last, at least in the ring. My brother never gave up easily, and he soon talked me into entering the boys' quarter-mile swim at the second annual Hudson River swim meet; I didn't win but I didn't drown either. I finished somewhere back in the pack. For a couple of years I hung on to the clipping about the race from the Yonkers *Herald Statesman* of 17 August 1935 just because my name showed up as an entrant. Next Richie tried to interest me in long distance running. He had been a successful runner in high school and on into his early twenties in a series of races in places like The Glen in Yonkers and Van Cortland Park in the Bronx. For years I had saved a clipping from the Yonkers paper when Richie beat the Olympic miler Joie Ray; although some might say it was somewhat late in Ray's career, it was still considered quite an accomplishment. Ray was the real thing; he had competed in three Olympic Games in the 1920s earning a bronze medal in 1924, and twice held the world record for the mile. Since I resembled Richie in build, he thought I might be a good match for the sport. He failed to consider the need for discipline in long distance running and I came up short in that department. He never really gave up on me, but one day he got married and moved away.

I was christened Michael Raymond but Richie always called me Raymond as did all the others who lived in our home while I was growing up; to the rest of the world I was Mike. Was this the source of some sort of "identity confusion" - or whatever the shrinks call it - later in my life? I don't know, maybe it was, even though at the time I understood why it happened. I was named after my Father's brother Michael. The problem was, he and his wife Jessie, with her Scottish burr, would visit frequently with their kids – one of whom was also named Mike - so someone started calling me by my middle name - Raymond - to distinguish me from the rest of the Mikes. It caught on and I answered to both names for the rest of my life.

I had a pleasant, quiet visit with my brother and his family in the village of Orono, just outside Bangor. Not satisfied with remaining a letter carrier the rest of his life, Richie had managed to get accepted into the highly competitive US Postal Inspection Service and, after six months of training in Washington DC and a year of internship in Vermont, he had been shipped off to Maine for his first regular assignment. It was an elite Corps within the US Postal Service at that time, with only 300 Inspectors across the country. The service was started by Ben Franklin when he was Colonial Postmaster General, and since then it has been the task of these plain-clothes agents to protect the mails. I realized it was a big-time job for a kid from Yonkers.

My brother's assignment in Maine involved the government's massive effort to set up the military mail system at the beginning of the war. It was a tough job, requiring him to make frequent trips by car between Bangor and Presque Isle through what must have seemed like Maine's endless winters. His job was considered essential to the war effort, and, although he never wore the uniform, he served his country just the same. The Post Office should have had the thanks of every GI who ever had a letter from home catch up with him in a foxhole.

I always felt Richie's wife, Anne, had mixed feelings about me. He said she thought I was a smart kid who should have been more serious about life and a little more accepting of authority. Maybe less of a wise-guy too. He said she was disappointed when I dropped out of high school; she felt I was wasting the talents God gave me. I think she gave up on me entirely in 1937 when the judge "suggested" that I either go back and finish high school or join the Army and I took the latter route. Anne was always pleasant to me when I was around but I don't think it would have broken her up if I wasn't around too much. Maybe she was afraid I'd be a bad influence on her kids or get drunk and be sick on the rug.

But now the brief vacation was over and it was time to get back to reality, my reality being to fly off to England and the war in a B-17. Before heading off across the Atlantic to end the war right away, we had stopped at Dow Army Air Field for maintenance and staging before our jump across the big pond. Our flight from the Crew Training Center in Nebraska had been pretty scenic, passing over the Great Lakes, parts of Canada, and straight into Dow Field where we would lay over for three days. We didn't have much to do at that point, so our pilot and CO, Lt Williams, had no hesitation in granting me a two-day pass to visit my brother and his family. As it turned out we were billeted right down the road from Orono, which happened to be where Richie and his family then lived - leaving me time for a quick visit and a glimpse of life with young kids in the house. As we said goodbye I couldn't help but wonder when I'd be seeing them – or any of my friends or relatives – again. But for me it was always "when", never "if".

We were starting to get used to long flights in the B-17 and we'd be doing nothing but long hauls from here on. Training for bombing missions involved hours of droning along at about 26,000 ft while our navigators tried to find the practice targets. These missions would be interrupted periodically by gunnery practice where us waist gunners – formally known as flexible gunners in B17s - would have the privilege of standing in our open windows with the subzero blasts at a couple of hundred miles per hour in our faces and letting off a few practice bursts with our .50 caliber Browning machine guns. Once in a while we would be provided with targets towed by a brave pilot, probably someone fresh out of training hoping to work his way out of some officer's doghouse, or sometimes towed by one of the brave volunteers of the Women Airforce Service

Pilots (WASP). Based on our accuracy levels I suspect they were able to use the targets repeatedly; I hope the pilots fared as well as the targets.

But I am getting ahead of myself; I should be telling you how I got to be an aerial gunner in the first place.

Chapter 5

Hawaii

I had been an Infantryman since my "decision" to enlist in 1937 and been moved around from New Jersey to Texas and then to California. Like all peacetime soldiers we had nothing to do but train; the amount of training you were "permitted" to do depended on your CO. We were lucky; we got a West Pointer who – like many officers at that time - had been stuck at the rank of Captain for twenty years. Rank was hard to come by for both officers and enlisted men in the peacetime Army from 1918 to 1941. Even Dwight Eisenhower took forever to advance from Second Lieutenant to Lieutenant Colonel, a rank he finally reached in 1936 - more than 21 years after graduating from West Point. Everything started speeding up after that. Even with the isolationists dragging their feet, the Army increased in numbers by 15-fold from 1939 to 1941. By then, Ike had been promoted to Brigadier General and, thanks to all the confusion in the rapidly expanding Army, I got to sew on my second stripe. Meanwhile, our CO saw to it that we stayed well trained for whatever enemy he thought was right around the corner.

Mike Henneberry (L) & Beatle Ames, May 1939

In the fall of 1941 our outfit was shipped to Hawaii to join the newly reorganized 25th Infantry Division. The Army had decided to strengthen the Hawaiian Department, as it was then called, to beef up the Islands' defenses. We were integrated with a newly-mobilized National Guard unit and spent our time training and trying to bring the citizen-soldiers up to speed. I had completed my first hitch by then, a four-year minority enlistment. Leaving the Army at that point was a definite consideration for me, given the lousy pay and lack of support from the American people – we were still wearing the tin hats and puttees from World War I for God's sake. But I must confess the Army had done a lot by way of straightening me out. I wasn't exactly a model citizen but I had kept my nose clean over the last four years and found out that books could be used for something besides paperweights. I learned to my surprise that history was a fascinating topic - even for a wise-guy from Yonkers. I was still only twenty-one and already I had grown up a little and had become a half-way decent soldier. And it was clear by then to most people in the military that we were heading for war so there was nothing to do but reenlist – if war actually came I'd be called back anyway.

We were stationed at Schofield Barracks about 20 miles from Honolulu when all hell broke loose that sleepy Sunday morning in December of 1941. As we streamed from the barracks in various stages of dress we could see aircraft flying close beside the Waianae Mountains - not through Kolekole Pass as they showed years later in the movies - and we could see smoke rising from nearby Wheeler Field. Our job was to defend the pass controlling access to the western part of Oahu against the anticipated enemy attack, so that was where we tried to get set up. Nobody ever showed up for us to shoot at, and that was a good thing since our weapons were locked in the arsenal and – believe it or not - the guy with the key wouldn't open it without written orders.

Although Schofield itself was not a direct target of the enemy attack, we took plenty of hits. In fact, the story has it that the first bomb of World War II fell near the Schofield barracks. Most of us did not have access to arms or ammunition, but some guys were able to get their hands on .30 caliber and .50 caliber machine guns and were firing at the low-flying planes from the roof and the balconies. By then we had seen the big red meatballs on the wings so we knew we had been attacked by Japan. Some new arrivals were in tents on the parade ground and made attractive targets for bombers that had already dropped their bombs and were looking for targets of opportunity on the way home. They seemed to think it was great sport - strafing helpless guys in pup tents. We took plenty of casualties that morning; the Schofield Hospital overflowed and stretchers were lined up outside the doors.

The scene at Wheeler Field was far more devastating; not many lives were lost but close to one hundred P-40s – lined up wingtip-to-wingtip - were destroyed because some genius decided they would be easier to guard all in a row than if they were returned to their protective revetments. Everyone knows about the losses the Navy took at Pearl Harbor, but our ability to fight a war in the air was blown away too. Between the attacks at Ford Island and Bellows, Hickham, and Wheeler Fields 188 US aircraft were lost that morning.

Living with the smoking wreckage all around us for the next few months made me realize that all our build-up of forces to defend the Hawaiian Islands could never have warded off the tragedy of Pearl Harbor for one simple reason: our strategic military planners were locked in the past. War would not just be fought on the ground or on the water anymore, it would be fought in the air as well. Gen. Billy Mitchell had spelled this out clearly in 1939 but the "old Army" wasn't listening.

All the preparations to defend Oahu belonged to the military of the past, an Army and Navy that assumed there would always be advance warning, there would always be time to disperse aircraft and unlock arsenals, and there would always be time to wait for the proper orders, preferably in writing. Extensive preparations had been made for the Japanese invasion that would follow the "softening-up" by air attacks without understanding that a coordinated attack at great distances was not likely since troop ships could never keep up with carriers. A sneak attack on a distant target would have to be from the air but, until 7 December 1941, our war planners were not used to looking to the sky.

Most people still don't realize it, but by the time of the Pearl Harbor attack we had already had many indications that Hawaii was vulnerable to attack and that the Japanese were a threat. Our ground forces on Oahu had been increased to more than 40,000 men by December of 1941 and the Island was thought to be well defended against the invasion that never came. Instead, as everyone knows, the surprise attack of 7 December nearly wiped out our Pacific Fleet. Roosevelt's "...date which will live in infamy" had come close to accomplishing its goal of eliminating our ability to fight in the Pacific. But the Japs made one mistake that December Sunday morning; as Admiral Yamamoto, the Commander of the sneak attack on Pearl Harbor is reported to have said: "I fear all we have done is awaken a sleeping giant and fill him with a terrible remorse". Whether he actually said it or it's just a line from a movie those were prophetic words.

Having been in Hawaii while history was being made had a lasting effect on me. Not only did it lead me to follow what was happening by reading newspapers and studying books about the history of our country, I suppose it also made me much more of a patriot than I had been. Our experience on Oahu on 7 December 1941 was enough to make any US soldier want to kill as many Japs as he could as soon as he could – which led me to the fateful decision to apply for one of the new Army Air Corps slots that were opening up as the United States started production of war machinery in quantities that, before it was over, would boggle the mind.

As a country, we were not at all well prepared for war in 1941 and not everyone favored our getting involved. In the summer of that year the House passed the extension of the existing draft law by a single vote. Although the "old Army" refused to accept the indications that wars from then on would be decided in the air, the political leadership and many senior Army Officers did see what was coming. The old Army Air Corps was redesigned and renamed and the new US Army Air Forces began an expansion the likes of which has never been seen before or since. Finally, someone in a position of authority started to listen to Billy Mitchell. In May of 1940 FDR called for the production of 50,000 planes; he upped the ante regularly until, in the three and a half years from Pearl Harbor to V-J day, American manufacturers turned out a total of about 296,000 aircraft, including 12,731 B-17s. Somehow, the Army

Air Forces had to provide trained crews for these planes – and that's where I came in.

With the rapid creation of new Air Force units, opportunities for old Regular Army guys to volunteer for flying duty became available. Having always been one who preferred a clean bed behind the lines to a muddy foxhole at the front, the first day the forms became available I hurried to fill out my application for a transfer to the Army Air Forces and assignment to aerial gunnery school, stressing what a good shot I was as a rifleman and somewhat exaggerating my experience with the Browning Automatic Rifle – the famed BAR that every infantryman learned to handle in those days. I thought I looked pretty good, on paper at least.

Chapter 6

Fort Myers

Many months went by and I was starting to think my application had found its way to the circular file, when one day out of the blue my orders arrived: I had been accepted into the Army Air Forces and assigned not to the aerial gunners school, but to the school for aerial gunnery instructors. Unfortunately for my plans to personally kill 100 Japs by Memorial Day, my weapons experience plus my two stripes and my status as Regular Army (RA) made me a natural for instructor duty.

Gunnery schools were just getting started late in 1941 as war became more and more probable. The first school was set up in Las Vegas and, by coincidence, took in its first students on 7 December 1941. These students were destined to be the first instructors as other new schools were set up around the country. The new schools were soon taking in thousands of students. The need for instructors became desperate and in July of 1942 a new school especially for training gunnery instructors was established at Buckingham Army Air Field near Fort Myers, Florida. My orders directed me to report to the first class at Buckingham, entering 7 September 1942. To my pleasant surprise, the orders also stated: "those successfully completing the Gunnery Instructors Course will be considered for promotion to the rank of sergeant". That wouldn't hurt the old paycheck.

There was nothing wrong with duty in Southwest Florida, at least after the hot and sticky summer was over, but we were kept too busy to care where we were. Which was a good thing. Buckingham Army Air Field was built from scratch on 6,500 acres, most of which was swampland that had to be drained. It has been referred to as the "ugliest Army AF field in the entire nation". But there was plenty of good flying weather and it was right next door to the Gulf of Mexico where we were not likely to bother anyone.

All the guys entering in my class had experience with weapons so we were able to get right to work. The Army's basic instructor training course was integrated smoothly into our training; even then the Army realized that we needed to know at least the basic elements of teaching before we were turned loose. Of course, everything we would be expected to teach about weapons and how to use them had to be included in our course too. All this was packed into six very intense weeks which, needless to say, went by very quickly. We had a weekend pass halfway through the course, but the only tourist things I can recall included an afternoon at the beach and a quick look at Thomas Edison's Winter Home in Fort Myers. Suddenly the course was over; we were not only Flexible Gunners but Gunnery School Instructors as well. Our last task was sewing on our new sergeant's stripes. The Army's attitude always was that if you completed a course you were eligible to teach it, so many of us were afraid we would be held at Buckingham to teach the Instructors Course we had just finished and a few guys did end up drawing that duty, but not me.

It always seemed that my next assignment was as far away as possible from my last one, and this time was no exception; from Fort Myers I was directed to travel by any available transportation to Kingman Aerial Flexible Gunnery School in Arizona reporting no later than 31 October 1942. That gave me seven days to travel to my new duty station and I had been in the Army long enough to know the hazards of arriving early. The biggest danger was that the First Sergeant, a member of a special breed that can't stand to see a man get any rest, would inevitably have a job that would "only take a couple of days" and "since you have time on your hands you are just the man for it"; the job comes with a guarantee that you will hate it. I always remembered the time in Hawaii when I was lucky enough to land the ever-popular job of inventorying the post uniform store. I still have nightmares about trying to match socks in pairs and never coming out even. Signing in to a new post at the last minute is definitely the safest bet.

I planned my trip from Florida to Arizona accordingly. A couple of buddies from our graduating class of brand-new aerial gunnery instructors were traveling by car from Fort Meyers to their new assignments at Tyndall Field in Florida's panhandle where they would join Gunnery School Number 9. They were only too happy to have me along as a passenger; not only would I pay for my share of the gas but by starting out with a full tank, carrying two full jerry-cans, and pooling all our gas rationing coupons we'd have enough fuel for the 500 mile trip with a few gallons left over. Sticking close to the national wartime speed limit of 35 miles an hour helped make the fuel last but I must confess we exceeded that speed limit more than once. Trips by car were a crap-shoot during the war; nobody had been able to buy a new car or even a new set of tires for the last couple of years and breakdowns and blow-outs were pretty common. All we could do was hope for the best. We figured we'd sign out from Fort Meyers just after midnight Friday and see how far we could get; with 3 guys sharing the driving and wartime traffic as light as it was, we pulled into Tyndall just after sunset that evening - but my buddies didn't sign in right away.

We decided to spend the next day exploring the beaches at Tyndall we had heard so much about.

The beaches lived up to their advance billing; the white sand edged by blue water seemed to go on forever in both directions. It was a Sunday with perfect beach weather so a pretty good crowd had turned out - mostly young people - late teens and early twenties - just what might be expected near a military base in those days. It was a pretty relaxed atmosphere - nobody had sewed his rank insignia on his bathing suit. I said "his" for a good reason; 95% of the people on the beach were guys. Pretty soon we found ourselves challenged to a volley ball game by three young guys: losers buy a case of beer the six of us would then consume. Even though they were all younger and taller what did we have to lose. Turned out a little closer than you might think; they were better at volleyball but we were better at cheating - but not that good. The young guys won handily. They were pretty good kids - fresh out of basic training and ready to start Aerial Gunnery School Monday morning. We polished off the case of Budweiser and decided to visit a little Mexican joint just a mile or two from the beach for some chow so all six of us piled into my buddy's car and off we went.

It's hard to mess up Mexican cooking so I didn't hear any complaints about the food - especially since we had started supplementing the beer with shots of tequila.

Nobody got roaring drunk but we had a few laughs and everyone seemed to enjoy our night out. Us "old guys" never told the kids we were instructors, just that we had recently earned our gunner's wings. They were content to pick our brains a little about what to expect. We ended the evening as old friends.

The three young guys had been classmates in high school in the Tampa area and had enlisted together. I wasn't sure their birth certificates would support the argument that they were old enough to enlist but that was none of my business so I didn't put anyone on the spot by asking. I was always good with names and faces and since my early days in the Army I kept a little notebook with names of guys I wouldn't mind seeing again and I decided to add these three young guys. The names David Grey, Mark Talbott and KG Younger Jr went into my book. As I worked my way through the notebook after the war I was unable to locate Grey or Talbott and I had reason to think they didn't survive the conflict; that was true of too many names in my book. I did locate KG Younger and we exchanged a couple of notes. He was eager to hear about my time in Stalag 17 and wanted to tell me about his 50 missions as an upper turret gunner in B-24s with the 15th Air Force over Italy. He had started out needing 25 missions to complete his tour of duty but as the war drew to a close and we gained air superiority and finally supremacy the required number kept creeping up. During a visit to

Seymour-Johnson Air Force Base in North Carolina in the late 1940s I traveled up to Durham for a long lunch with KG. By then he was at Duke University on a football scholarship. We had both changed a lot in appearance, but we picked up the conversation right where we left it five years earlier. We exchanged a couple of post cards after that but eventually we lost touch. He turned up again in the newspapers some years later when he became CEO of a major trucking company; I always figured he'd turn out OK.

I still had plenty of time left to get to Arizona and I decided to spend one more day at Tyndall and store away a few more memories of those beaches. I was on my own for the day since my buddies signed in that morning and were already in an instructors' orientation course. It was just me and the sun and the sand that day, then I had to start paying attention to my trip west. It seemed as though everything in America was on the move by that time and I had no trouble finding a very hard seat on a C-47 heading directly from Tyndall to Las Vegas and from there a quick train ride down to Kingman. Although the school was in the middle of nowhere it was easy to get to; the Sante Fe railroad ran right past the base and there was a stop about half a mile away from the front gate. It was time to go to work.

Chapter 7

Kingman, Arizona

The Kingman Flexible Gunnery School had been set up in a remote area of the Mohave Desert at a cost of nine million dollars in the summer of '42 and it was ready to start taking in students by December of the same year. Before the war was over two and a half years later, more than 36,000 flexible gunners were trained at Kingman. During my stay there we were pretty proud of our ability to turn green civilians into competent gunners in a matter of weeks, and we had few complaints from the field about the competence level of our grads.

Most of the instructors assigned to Kingman and the other Gunnery Schools were civilians a few months earlier and had no experience with weapons before entering the Army. Although only 22 years old, as a newly-minted Gunnery Instructor I already fit the description of an "old soldier" by the standards of the "new Army". As a "reward" my duties would involve not only teaching a group of my own but also supervising a handful of new soldier-instructors as well – additional duty I could have done without. For the next few months our efforts were focused on building the AAF's fourth Flexible Gunners Training School on a barren patch of desert in the middle of nowhere and at the same time getting ready for our first classes. We were open for business before the end of 1942. One of the things the Japs hadn't counted on was the way we Americans could "hurry up" when we had to.

Few of the students entering the various gunnery schools around the country had any experience with guns of any sort. One glance was enough to prove these guys were civilians in khaki. Most of them had been in the Army for only a matter of weeks and before basic training had never seen a gun up close in their lives. Anticipating this, the AAF designed the gunnery course to start at the most basic level possible, and nothing could be more basic than learning to shoot a BB gun. Initially, Daisy provided the model 140 air rifle, the military versions of the famous "Red Ryder" carbine for this purpose, but only 30,000 of them were delivered before Daisy had to shut down production because they couldn't get their hands on the steel they needed, steel being eaten up in huge quantities by war machinery like planes, ships, and tanks. Needless to say, a requisition for steel to make BB guns did not command the highest priority in 1942.

Before long, the .22 cal Range was set up at Kingman and equipped with weapons that superficially resembled the weapons found in AAF aircraft at the time but they fired a small, relatively quiet, and inexpensive bullet. With its rifled barrel, the .22 was much more accurate and had more range than the BB gun and so it provided a more realistic training situation. This method of teaching proved to be very effective, permitting the students to learn the "sight picture" and to avoid or rid themselves of many of the bad habits novice shooters develop. From there, students moved to shotguns which, at first, helped them get used to the noise and recoil of a more powerful weapon. Later, they moved to the skeet range, shooting clay pigeons with shotguns to introduce them to the concept of hitting a moving target.

To those who have never tried it – which included almost all the Army Brass in 1942 – hitting one aircraft from another one seemed like a relatively straight-forward problem. Even when it was pointed out that the situation was complicated by the fact that both the target aircraft and the gun platform were moving, usually in different directions and at different rates of speed, the Brass did not appreciate the difficulty of the task. After all, one moving tank – in the right hands – had no trouble hitting another tank moving at a different speed and in a different direction.

It was hard to make the case that hitting a target in three dimensions was a new and different problem. The point is, a major new skill had to be mastered – even for the most experienced machine gunner it is a whole different story hitting a moving target when you both are moving in three dimensions and in different directions. We didn't have any sophisticated equipment designed for the purpose of learning that skill at that point in the war, but some creative minds at Kingman hit on a solution for the problem of getting practice in hitting a moving target from a moving platform by placing students in the back of a pick-up truck and having them shoot at clay pigeons as they rode by the skete range. This and other novel methods of instruction used at Kingman were apparently quite successful; Kingman teams were frequent winners in morale-boosting competitions between Gunnery Schools.

Synthetic Trainers also played an important role in gunnery training. Most students had the chance to hone their skills on the so-called "Jam Handy", a relatively simple device that projected outlines of aircraft on a screen for the student who fired a gun-like device containing a camera which scored his performance. Although the name suggests it might refer to the plague of all gunners – jamming - it was actually named for its inventor, Henry Jamison "Jam" Handy, an Olympic swimmer who had become a leader in the field of audio and video communications. Specializing in training films for operators of industrial equipment before the war, he switched to developing training films for operators of military equipment in WWI. He did the same thing for the next war; his company produced more than 7,000 training films for the military during WWII. At Kingman we had a special sound-proof building designed for the Jam Handy. Sixteen Jam Handy trainers were set up at Kingman by February 1943 and remained in use throughout the war. They provided some much needed diversity in the training program and were, all in all, quite effective. The Jam Handy building also turned out to be the perfect spot for Saturday night movies to entertain the troops.

The Waller trainer – a more sophisticated Synthetic Trainer also based on film but using panoramic screens with actual footage of aerial combat – arrived later but, as we shall see, I had been transferred by then. I heard later that these devices were especially helpful in introducing gunners to the infamous Pursuit Curve – in this case the flight path followed by a fighter as it closes on a bomber. In the early stages of the war, before the introduction of more sophisticated gun sights, it was like trying to solve a calculus problem in your head. The trouble was most of us had never heard of calculus at that point.

The base library opened in March of 1943 and was initially stocked with more than 800 books, everything from Zane Gray Westerns to basic science texts. The Army was well aware of the fact that, while the choice of sites for the Kingman Flexible Gunners School was perfect for the purpose, it left a lot of soldiers in the middle of nowhere without an enemy to shoot at and with little or nothing to do. There was always plenty of 3.2 beer, and regular movies helped, as did the USO Canteen. As you can imagine, Army training films on such engaging topics as dental hygiene and venereal diseases were always a big hit too. Probably the most popular events with the troops were the touring entertainers who gave their time and efforts to bolster our morale. I can clearly remember the afternoon in March of '43, several months after the first class of students arrived at Kingman, when Bob Hope and his show came to the School. Jerry Colonna and Martha Raye and some others I've forgotten were with him and I thought the troops would never let them quit.

A few months later Kay Kyser, the "Ol' Professor of Swing", brought his popular band to the base. His music was right up there at the top of my list. I was not a musician, but I had developed a keen interest in the Big Band music of the '30s and even thought I might look into becoming a radio "Disk Jockey" after the war. I had often been told I had the gift of gab, and I was also a pretty good mimic, doing all the usual imitations of Bogart, Cagney, Gable and other Hollywood stars. Anyway, about a month later, as I recall, another touring show came through; there were rumors that the laughter could be heard all the way to the Grand Canyon before "The Three Stooges" were done with us.

Kingman also had separate clubs for instructors and students, mainly to provide a much needed refuge for instructors to get away from the students and let our hair down a little. In those days in the Army a three-striper was called a Sergeant but was not considered an NCO, and so was not welcome at the NCO Club. At most posts the lower enlisted ranks had a club of their own but at the aerial gunnery schools there was also an additional facility just for instructors and we usually gathered there after duty for a cold beer and a rehash of our day's adventures on the range.

I was always surprised by the level of camaraderie among soldiers isolated together, especially in a stressful situation. Hard-nosed guys you could never picture getting sentimental when you worked with them out on the range would get misty-eyed in a hurry when Dinah Shore would come on the jukebox in the Club. Singing drinking songs with military themes was one of the main activities at Kingman's clubs – as it was in every US Officer's Club, NCO Club and Airmen's Club all over the world. Every club has an upright piano, never new and always a little out of tune. Then there is the piano player. Somehow there always is one. He was strictly a volunteer and he always materialized mysteriously after everyone had his second beer. And I always found it mysterious that everyone knew the words to all those songs we had never heard before. And it was funny how everyone could suddenly carry a tune.

The songs we sang the most didn't come from Irving Berlin or Johnny Mercer and they could be described as pretty juvenile – but if you had been there you wouldn't say that. We are talking about guys barely out of their teens whose lives have suddenly been placed on hold. They might have started their careers in the butcher shop or the corner gas station or been off to their first year of college, but now they had kissed the girlfriends goodbye; now they belonged to Uncle Sam and were in for the duration. They had no idea where they would be sent or what they would be asked to do. We all knew a lot of us would not be coming back, so underlying everything was an unspoken fear. Most young men deal with fear by acting as though they are immortal and ridiculing – on the surface at least - the things they fear the most. A lot of the songs we sang were based on that kind of thinking. Saturday night never got very old before the rafters of the Club would reverberate with a favorite tune with verses like this one:

"There was blood upon the risers
There was blood upon the chute,
And the end of his intestine
was a'hanging from his boot.
Gory, Gory Hallelujah, Gory ...."

You know the tune.

The part of the gunnery problem overlooked by the Brass was the three-dimensional nature of aerial combat. Fighters attacking bombers were not only much faster and more maneuverable but, by knowing the mounting positions of the guns on the bombers, they were able to "hide" in positions where the bomber's guns could not reach them. Unavoidably, the extent of motion available to aircraft-mounted guns was limited. These were problems that could only be learned from experience in the air, and after mastering the basics with .22s, shotguns, and static-mounted machine guns, gunnery students finally were airborne.

Initially, we used the venerable North American Texan trainer, the two-seater every pilot of that era learned to fly in. It was known to the AAF as the AT-6 (the Navy called it the NJ-1) and for gunnery training it was fitted with a machine gun in the back seat; it provided the first at least partly realistic experience for gunnery students. The AT-6 was not stressed for the .50 caliber machine guns found in bombers, but plenty of valuable experience shooting at targets towed by other aircraft was had with .30 caliber machine guns mounted in the back seat of an AT-6. However, it was a big step from the AT-6 to the B-17. It had been decided back in January of '43 that the Flexible Gunnery School at Kingman would train gunners for B-17s exclusively. And everyone agreed that there was no substitute for training in actual aircraft. The trouble was there were not enough B-17s to go around. Understandably, there was great demand for the aircraft from operational units fighting wars in Europe and the Pacific and from pilot training units here in the states. Gunnery School was not near the top of the priority list.

But finally the B-17s began to arrive and the training program suddenly became more realistic. A few months earlier we had had our first good look at a B-17 when the famous *"Memphis Bell"* stopped at Kingman while on a bond tour of the country after becoming the first American Bomber recognized for completing 25 missions into Germany without the loss of life. (Not everyone agrees that the *Memphis Belle* was first, but that's another story). The *Memphis Belle's* pilot, Major Robert Morgan, and most of his original crew stayed at Kingman for 2 days and we had the chance to pick their brains about the aircraft, combat missions, and life in England. But now we had a few aircraft of our own and we would actually get our hands on weapons capable of going to war.

The morale of the Instructor Corps had never been good but with the arrival of the B-17s it sunk even further. None of us had volunteered for instructor duty; we had signed up to go to war and we were constantly frustrated as we watched our graduates draw combat assignments while we turned around to meet another incoming class. Now, after a week of transition training in real live B-17s to qualify us to teach more guys on their way to war, we were feeling even more sorry for ourselves and what seemed like permanent state-side duty. Sure, the needs of the service come first but we weren't interested in hearing that again and morale among instructors was sinking pretty low.

Surprisingly, the Air Forces bureaucracy recognized this as a real problem and early in 1943 started permitting instructors to apply for combat duty after 6 months on the job; it was probably assumed that – in typical Army fashion – it would take six months for reassignments to start coming through so most guys would actually do a year of instructor duty. We were pretty happy with the idea, and we had to admit some reasonable thinking had gone into the decision; a small percentage of the graduates in each gunnery class would be sent to a new, abbreviated course at the Buckingham Instructors School and then back to their original school to replace us guys foolish enough to volunteer to get shot at. This turn-over was very effective in boosting morale, with the enthusiasm of the new blood and everyone's realization that they wouldn't be stuck in the job until the war ended. Needless to say, I was at the front of the line to get my transfer papers in.

My reassignment orders arrived so quickly I began to wonder if someone at Kingman was eager to be rid of me. My CO assured me over a farewell bucket of beer that this was not the case; I had volunteered for combat when originally applying for transfer to the Army Air Corps and I was also one of the first instructors assigned to Kingman, so I was among the first to be shipped out. He reluctantly wished me good luck; he had been trying to get a combat assignment himself since the war began and confessed he was more than a little envious.

So here I was, less than six years since opting for the soldier's life rather than that of the high school student. If you had met me in 1937 it wouldn't have taken you long to realize that here was a young man with a chip on his shoulder. In fact, my typical wise crack in those days was that I was very well balanced – I had a chip on each shoulder! But that was when I was 17. Now I was 23 and I had grown up a lot – the Army had seen to that. I never got in any serious trouble as a soldier, but I did draw a lot of K.P. in the early days as I learned my lessons more slowly than a lot of guys. One tough old sergeant – who had just barely finished eight grade himself and made no bones about it – convinced me to get my GED which wasn't a very hard thing to do once I put my mind to it. This made me an official high school graduate and the Army didn't care how I got that way. The old timer sold me on the idea by pointing out that when I came up for promotion I didn't want to be competing against a lot of guys who had a leg up on me. The long and short of it was I had found a home in the Army and now I was going to start earning my pay in a dead serious manner.

Chapter 8

Crossing the Big Pond

The next few months went by in a blur after my orders arrived in mid-July, 1943. I was directed to report immediately to Kearney Army Air Force Base in Nebraska to join one of many new B-17 crews being assembled there. Kearney had recently been designated a Bombardment Processing and Crew Training Center. After assignment to a crew we would undergo a brief orientation course specifically for B-17s, then pick up a new, factory-fresh aircraft and spend a few weeks getting the bugs out of airplane and crew. Next we would ferry it to England and turn it over to the Bomber Replacement Depot. Then we would be sent to the Crew Processing Center for a few days of ground school while we waited our assignment to a bomber squadron. I guess you could call that trip a shake-down cruise for both airplane and crew. Things were moving at a pretty fast pace by then and I started to realize that the Big Event wasn't far away: I had been in the Army six years at that point without ever firing a shot in anger, and now I was being sent off to kill somebody.

Incidentally, the goal of the Army Air Forces at that time was to make sure that all air crew members had the rank of Staff Sergeant or better. Some of this may have been for motivational purposes but I think most of it was to ensure that anyone captured by the enemy was a Commissioned Officer or a Non-Commissioned Officer (NCO). The Geneva Convention of 1929, covering the treatment of prisoners of war, stipulated that Officers and NCOs could not be required to perform manual labor. In any event, I got to pin on my fourth stripe and I finally got to go to the NCO club. As it would turn out, sewing on that 4th stripe was a life-and-death matter in many cases including my own.

By the time I arrived at Kearney our crew was already partly assembled with Lieutenant Walter Williams assigned as our pilot and Commanding Officer. Lt Williams, from Minnesota, was my age; he had gone right from college graduation into pilot training as a cadet, and by the time he reached Kearney he had a total of about 320 hours flying time - about 20 of which was in the B-17. I had been around long enough to know that was not much time at the controls of an aircraft, but I also knew it was not unusually low for a new bomber pilot at this stage of the war. With the small number of pilots on hand when hostilities broke out, the rate at which they were being lost in combat, and the number of new aircraft rolling off the production lines the demand for new pilots was unbelievable. There was no time to turn kids into seasoned veterans before they were sent into combat.

Our co-pilot, Lt Belford Candler from New Jersey, was a couple of months younger and had about the same amount of flying time as Lt Williams. Scuttlebutt had it that Lt Williams was chosen as the head of our crew over Lt Candler because of date-of-rank; he had been commissioned a week before Lt Candler. As it turned out, they both settled into their jobs and seemed to get along very well; they were both pretty good guys and I would have been happy to serve under either one.

The day I arrived at Kearney I ran into S/Sgt Al Wickline in processing which, in the Army, is another word for waiting forever in a big room with a lot of other guys until someone stumbles across a form you have to sign to get paid. Wickline, from Ohio, was another "prior service" guy like me; we had known each other slightly at Kingman when he was a gunnery student and we were both surprised to learn that we were assigned to the same combat crew, with him as tail gunner and me as right waist gunner. So I knew someone to have a beer with right off the bat.

B-17s at that stage of the war had ten crew members, four officers and six enlisted men. Within the next 24 hours our crew was complete with the assignment of Lt Carl Abele from Ohio as Navigator and Lt Tom Breen from Long Island as Bombardier. T/Sgt Tom Hanrahan from Philly was our radio operator; M/Sgt Clyde Bush from South Dakota was our top turret gunner; S/Sgt Bill Genette from Detroit manned the ball turret; and S/Sgt Jim Deese from Georgia was right beside me as our left waist gunner. It seems strange to think about this now, but when our crew was fully assembled we had no one younger than 20 and no one older than 24. But this wasn't so unique then; what everyone seems to have forgotten is that our war was largely fought by guys barely out of their teens. Our crew started getting to know each other but we didn't have much time to devote to it. The B-17 orientation course lasted five pretty intensive days, and then we were introduced to the aircraft we would ferry to the European Theatre of Operations (ETO) – a brand new B-17 fresh off the Boeing assembly line and flown to Kearney by a WASP (again, more about them later).

Early in 1943 Dow Army Air Field (now Bangor International Airport) began staging heavy bombers and getting them ready for the trip to England or Africa. In the course of the war 10,500 bombers went through Dow Field on their way to war. During our stay at Dow we learned we had been assigned to one of the North Atlantic air ferry routes which would take us from Maine to Goose Bay, Laborador to Reykjavik, Iceland to Prestwick, Scotland. One topic of conversation was the fact that we would be flying a "great circle route" very similar to the one Charles Lindbergh had flown on his legendary trip to Paris just 16 years earlier. Of course, unlike "Lucky Lindy" we would have the luxury of two stops along the way. B-17s were not particularly fast airplanes. Although top speed was a respectable 300 mph, normal cruise - a compromise between performance and fuel economy - was only 170 mph. Just as with the automobile, aircraft fuel mileage can be improved, within limits, by operating more slowly; at 170 mph a B-17 had a range of about 2,800 miles without accounting for the effect of winds so theoretically a nonstop flight from Maine to Scotland was feasible - but not in the plan. In any event, four days after our arrival in Maine we were on our way across the Atlantic.

I had become interested in technical and mechanical things when I was a kid following my brothers around while they experimented with the latest things like crystal radios and cigar boxes with batteries, bulbs and wires. When I was 16 my brother Richie bought his first car - a used 1935 Ford. It was the first car in the family and I got to drive it a few times while I was learning. I guess if it had been mine I would have taken it apart a little at a time just to see how it worked and put it back together again just to see if I could do it. My mechanical interest came in handy in learning about the workings of all the weapons I was exposed to during my early years in the Army. An old story in the Army is how you have to learn to field strip your weapon and reassemble it in the dark; that sort of thing was never a problem for me, and I was pretty quick at it. Now here I was flying across the Atlantic Ocean in the most sophisticated mechanical device man had yet invented. Since arriving at Kearney I had made a game out of learning what made the Flying Fortress tick. Some of what I'm writing here I learned during the war but a lot of it came from things I read when the war was over and I had plenty of time on my hands.

The B-17 was the best known airplane during the war even though a lot more B-24s were produced. This was partly because pilots and crews preferred the B-17 over the B-24 and so it got a better press. There were good reasons the B-17 was preferred since it was a safer airplane; there were plenty of statistics showing that your chances of getting home in a B-17 were much better than in a B-24 and all the crew members knew all about this by the middle of the war. Politics at home and abroad led to the parallel production of both aircraft in the first place, and kept the B-24 production lines rolling although US commanders in the field - especially the legendary Jimmy Doolittle - were outspoken about their preferences. The RAF preference for the B-24 as a night bomber, plus its greater bomb load and longer range, kept new B-24s rolling out of US factories. But lots of B-17s were made and they were the favorites of the VIII Bomber Command/8th Air Force bombing Europe out of England. Before the war ended, I later learned, 12,732 B-17s were produced, peaking at 16 aircraft per day in April of 1944. Boeing, which designed the plane, made most of them but Douglas and Lockheed Vega made a few as well. For comparison, 18,431 B-24s were made during its production lifetime.

Looking back at it, the job of getting all these planes into the hands of the people who knew what to do with them was an unbelievably complex problem, second only to the complexity of producing them all in the first place. I would not have wanted to be the Lt Colonel who had to explain to the generals in the Pacific why the generals in Europe got more planes than they did last month or vice versa. The Army Air Forces were using several ways of getting aircraft to England at that point in the war but still found it impossible to meet the demand. Some bombers were shipped over on transport ships and reassembled over there, but that was obviously an inefficient process and didn't last long. Ferrying – flying the aircraft under its own power – was the most common method of delivering planes from the US to England, and we would be the guys to do the ferrying of one each B-17. In any given bomb group there was a discrepancy between the need for bombers and the need for crews. Although the need for both was staggering, the need for planes was greater. Lots of times a crew limped home in a terminally-ill bomber;

the crew survived while the bomber did not, so you had a crew in need of a new plane. That's why crews and planes were distributed through two separate pipelines and that's why we had to hand over that shiny new model when we got to Scotland and get in another queue for replacement crews.

The concept of delivering newly manufactured aircraft by flying them to their destination had been adopted before WWII broke out in Europe and was continuously refined as circumstances changed. At one point American civilian pilots in the employ of the British delivered planes from the factories to drop-off points in Canada and the RAF took them from there. With the onset of the Lend-Lease program the number of planes bound for Europe ramped up sharply and in 1941 the US Army Air Corps Ferrying Command was established; with a drastically expanded mission it became the Air Transport Command (ATC) a year later. The Ferrying Command stayed in business as a division of ATC; by the end of the war it had ferried 267,000 aircraft to their combat units. Obviously, the demand for pilots for every kind of duty including ferrying was tremendous as the US entered into WWII. There never were enough pilots to go around until the war was almost over. The strategy for getting aircraft from the factories to the various combat theaters was to fly the planes via a domestic network to the jumping-off points where an overseas network took over. To help alleviate the pilot shortage, the US took the surprisingly sensible approach of approving the Women Airforce Service Pilots (WASP) program which accepted volunteers, put them through the same pilot training the men received, and put them to work in a few odd jobs like transporting cargo and towing targets as I mentioned, but mostly ferrying planes from the factory to the jumping-off points – but no further.

The Women Airforce Service Pilots (WASP) were never permitted to ferry planes to overseas destinations even when the shortage of pilots was drastic, but they played a major role in delivering aircraft domestically. Before being disbanded in 1944, 1,037 WASP (N.B. "WASP" is correct usage; the "P" stands for pilots) flew 12,600 missions in 78 different types of aircraft. But the treatment of these brave pilots was a national disgrace. Although trained by the Army; paid by the Army; suited up in Army uniforms; and sent off to do some of the Army's toughest jobs they were never officially part of the Army. They were never permitted to fly in combat, but 38 WASP died in aviation accidents in the line of duty. To our nation's shame, these pilots were denied military funerals – they were not members of the military, were they? The Army didn't even have the decency to cover the costs of their burials. The War Department refused to provide flags for their coffins – something every soldier is entitled to. Congress denied military benefits for WASP in 1944 – no free college education on the GI bill for them! Thirty-three years later Congress recognized the small-mindedness of its predecessors and approved veteran's benefits for the surviving WASP – probably thinking it would not cost them much at that late date; veterans were less inclined to go to college in their 50's! By then it was 1977 - the same year the modern US Air Force graduated its first women pilots.

Where would you like it delivered?

Some history student should write a thesis exploring the motivation behind this shoddy treatment of this small group of brave women who contributed mightily to the war effort.

But here I am in England. After dropping off our ferried chariot we endured an endless and boring train ride to the Crew Assignment Depot near London. In the best military manner what we did next was wait. While waiting we were treated to such popular all-day lectures as "Personal Hygiene in a Combat Zone" or "Escaping from the Germans if Shot Down". Maybe I should have paid more attention to the last one.

As we knew it would, our "permanent" assignment finally came through: VIII Bomber Command (soon to become the 8th Air Force) 384th Bomb Group, 544th Squadron, stationed at AAF Station 106 at Grafton Underwood, Northamptonshire, East Midlands. (52 degrees 24 minutes 0 seconds N by 0 degrees 38 minutes 0 seconds W.) Finally we were off to see what fate had in store for us.

384th Bomb Group

544th Squadron

Chapter 9

Grafton Underwood

By the time we caught up with the 544th squadron at Grafton Underwood on 3 September 1943 it had been in place for several months and had things pretty well organized. We had a place to eat, a place to sleep, and the latrine was in working order – what more could we want? The Group's ground echelon had an interesting trip from the States; they traveled by truck, train, and ship, crossing the Atlantic on the Queen Elizabeth and arriving in England on 2 June 1943, almost a week after the 384th's aircraft arrived. The trip was peppered with exciting episodes such as a storm at sea that caused substantial crowding at the rail, and an intercepted message reporting that their ship had been sunk two days out of New York. They hadn't noticed sinking, so they kept on sailing.

Grafton Underwood AAF Station 106 had been in US hands since we became involved in the war. It was the first base available for American bombers and hosted several different bomb groups before the 384th arrived in May of 1943 and stayed until the end of the war. Shortly before we arrived the 384th had staked a claim to dropping the first US bomb of WWII on German soil. Like every other combat unit sending bombers across the channel to fight the enemy, the 384th took significant losses and replacement planes and crews were constantly arriving. Our Squadron - the 544th - was widely known as the "Ghost Squadron". In the summer of 1943, on a bombing raid on Hamburg, all seven ships of the 544th failed to return. The entire squadron was lost that day.

It didn't take much time hanging around with the 384th Group's experienced crews to realize that morale was very low. The Group had taken very heavy losses on the Schweinfurt raid on 17 August and the crews didn't see any positive changes in the wind. In fact, the entire VIII Bomber Command had taken unsustainable losses and morale was at an all-time low in all the Groups. Scuttlebutt had it that despite the losses the raid was fairly effective and the Brass believed a follow-up raid could provide a knock-out punch to Schweinfurt's ball bearing factories. The rumor mill also had it that the second raid would have to wait while Bomber Command replenished its crews and planes but that it would probably take place before the end of the year. This mission was a grim prospect facing the crews that would have to fly it and nobody was happy about the idea.

On a more pleasant note, AAF Station 106 did own the bragging rights for a few notable figures who passed through before our arrival. Paul Tibbetts, later the pilot of the "Enola Gay" that dropped the world's first atomic bomb on Hiroshima in 1945, had led the first US raid to the continent from Grafton-Underwood. Also, Clark Gable, the actor, was a frequent visitor to the station. I can't resist throwing in a few words about Gable because he was an aerial gunner like me. Gable's wartime adventures began on 16 January 1942 just a few weeks after Pearl Harbor. Gable's wife, the actress Carole Lombard, was killed in a tragic plane crash at age 33; she was returning from a trip promoting the sale of War Bonds when her plane crashed into Mount Potosi 30 miles southwest of Las Vegas. A few months later Gable enlisted in the Army and requested assignment to gunnery school looking for combat duty. However, Hap Arnold, Commanding General of the AAF, unable to pass up the publicity value of Hollywood's leading actor, sent him to OCS with the promise of a "special aerial gunner's assignment" after he was commissioned. Arnold kept his promise but Gable was not too happy to find that his special assignment was to produce a combat-based film designed to recruit aerial gunners. In preparation for the movie, Gable went through Gunnery School at Tyndall Field and earned his aerial gunner's wings. While working on the movie with the 351st Bomb Group Gable kept putting himself in harms way, eventually flying five combat missions and earning the Air Medal and the Distinguished Flying Cross. He tried for more combat assignments, but MGM, aware of his drawing power at the box office - which could only have been enhanced by his wartime service - had enough political clout to insure Gable was kept far away from any further action.

Gable, of course, wasn't the only famous Hollywood star to serve in the 8th AAF. James Stewart was a B-17 instructor who then went to Europe to fly 20 missions in B-24s; he stayed in the reserves after the war and reached the rank of general. And there were other celebrities too numerous to count who did their bit in WWII. For one example, former NY Giants defensive back and Dallas Cowboys Head Coach Tom Landry was a B-17 pilot for 30 combat missions in the 860th Bombardment Squadron in Europe. He survived a crash landing that sheared off both wings of his bomber; after that, football probably seemed pretty tame to him.

As soon as we staked out a bunk in the Nissen Hut that served as our barracks, unloaded our gear, and checked the latest rumors we set off to find out how a combat unit works. Two other replacement crews arrived the same day and we all sat through the standard new - arrival briefing. We soon learned we were queued up for the next available "Flying Fortress" but it would probably be several weeks before any planes would be available. There was plenty to do in the meantime. The officers would start right away flying missions as temporary members of other crews, first as observers and then filling their regular roles. This would give them an introduction to squadron procedures and the local geography as well as some exposure to operating in a combat environment. Just the procedures for forming up as a strike force for a mission were complex enough to require a short course of in-flight tutoring. Enlisted crew members were treated more casually when it came to flying missions before being assigned to an aircraft. For the officers it was a structured deal to make sure they all had some missions under their belts before they were sent off with all the responsibility for their own plane and crew but the enlisted men were thought to be better off flying their first mission with the crew members they knew and trusted.

While we waited, the gunners had plenty to learn about the ways guns were handled locally; they were stored wrapped in heavy, oily rags to prevent corrosion - something we hadn't had to worry about in Arizona. Before a mission they had to be cleaned and lightly oiled and after the mission they had to be cleaned and wrapped again for storage. We also learned that the bolts were removed from the guns when the planes were parked. Each gunner was responsible for his guns' bolts and many guys carried them around in their pockets all the time in fear of forgetting them and taking off with guns that couldn't be fired.

Newly arrived NCOs - they might have been called "Kids in Stripes" - were sent into combat as needed. I guess the Brass didn't want us to have a lot of time to sit around and wonder and worry about it. Some replacements arrived independently rather than as members of a crew and they were assigned to existing crews as required so some gunners were in the air firing at the enemy a few days after arriving at the station. The enlisted members of our crew remained together as a unit; we had been warned that we might be called upon to fill an individual gap when an established crew had a sudden vacancy but it never happened to any of us. When we were not working we spent plenty of time talking about the first combat experience and concluded that the guy who tells you he isn't scared is almost certainly lying. We agreed that the first exposure to actual combat was bound to be an exercise in sheer terror for most people no matter what the preparation. Some men handle it better than others. Hemingway said it best: "Courage is grace under pressure". The problem is you don't know how you will handle it until you get there. Several things seemed remarkable to me while I was in England. First, it was remarkable how so many regular guys who had never before left their hometowns, had never before flown in an airplane, and had never before fired any kind of a weapon became seasoned warriors in a matter of months. But even more remarkable to me was that so many guys were able to control their fear.

There was plenty to be learned, but since we were not flying missions yet we had more free time than we would have later. On our third day at Station 106 a new Group Commander, Col Julius Lacey, took over. We had the chance to suit up in our best Class A uniforms and march around in the mud for a Change of Command Ceremony. We began to understand why the Station was usually referred to as "Grafton Undermud"; unlike the US Brass, Britain's military masterminds didn't always position their airfields with the best flying weather in mind! Mixing with the new crowd, one of the first things I noticed was that a favorite topic of conversation was the number of missions a flyer had completed; survive 25 missions with the VIII Bomber Command and you got to go home. I first heard about this when the *"Memphis Belle"* visited Kingman but now it became personal. As a guy got closer to the magic number his buddies stopped mentioning it and the tension grew. There was no competition here; everyone pulled for everyone else to make it through but a lot of guys didn't. The probability of making 25 wasn't good but I tried not to think about that; I figured one at a time was the way to keep your head on straight. I had shot enough craps to know that even if you threw snake eyes 5 times in a row the probability that you would throw it again didn't change; if you flipped a coin and it came up heads five times in a row the probability that it would be heads next time was still 50%. So I figured I would take it one mission at a time, even though I knew the probability of coming back from any mission was averaging less than 50%. Which brings up the worst aspect of war of any kind: watching your friends go down. I heard many a story from guys who watched close friends get blown out of the sky in an instant death or saw a buddy's plane spinning straight down with no chutes appearing. Coming back to the barracks to find several empty bunks was a common occurrence. I'm not sure this is worse than an infantryman having his buddy die in his arms, but there is nothing good to be said for it in either case. Before we started flying missions of our own - like all the ground personnel - we got in the habit of waiting for the Squadron to return from a mission and counting the planes as they came into view. I don't remember a day when they all came back.

With our role of also serving as we stood and waited for a new B-17, day-passes were not hard to get and we were able to spend some time exploring the English countryside. The village of Grafton Underwood was tiny by anyone's standards with just a handful of buildings and a population of only 99 people. Fortunately for the bomber crews, many of whom found religion to go with their new line of work, there was the beautiful 1,000 year-old Church of Saint James the Apostle as the central attraction in the village. It did a brisk business every day of the week. But everyone needs a little recreation, and guys with passes were usually hauled by special "buses" – the Army's famous

2.5 ton "Deuce-and-a-Half" truck – to the nearby village of Kettering west of the air base. If no trucks were available the troops walked the 4 miles, helped along by the motivation of a few pints on the way out and the First Sergeant's wrath on the way back.

If we expected to be received with open arms by the Brits, we were in for a surprise. They seemed torn between being annoyed that we hadn't arrived sooner and being miffed that the "colonists" actually thought they could bail out the British Empire. They knew all about us from Hollywood movies and American music and they imitated our songs, our slang, and our mannerisms - but that didn't mean they had to like us. In a land where handguns were rare, they couldn't understand a country where everyone carried a gun – they knew all about that from American movies. But it all worked out in the end. The Brits couldn't help but notice that the war began to turn around soon after we arrived in England and they started resenting us a little less. And it didn't take us Yanks long to figure out that England really was worth defending. After all, how can a country be all bad where even the smallest village has at least one pub?

There were clubs on the base where we could usually get a wartime version of a beer but whenever liberty could be had it was off to Kettering and straight for the pubs. England seemed a strange country to us. Most of its businesses were open only a few hours a day. The pubs were especially mystifying with their "hours" that made no sense and it seemed strange to hear the cry of "time, gentlemen, time" in the middle of the afternoon - telling us to drink up. We soon caught on to the way the natives coped with such nonsense: they ordered three rounds just before the pumps shut down and "drank up" at their leisure. Being Yanks, we learned the customs fast enough and soon became used to strange hours, sudden interruptions, and slightly warm beer.

Of course, being healthy, red-blooded American boys - and I do mean boys, with an average age in the Squadron very close to 20 - the troops were interested in more than just a few pints but in general the local women were cooler than the beer, at least toward the Yanks crowding their pubs. A few guys had some luck with the ladies but they were usually the dance-floor show-offs. Most of us could never understand why a guy could be uglier than sin, but the girls would still go for him if he danced like a fool. Such is life. The fact is us GIs outnumbered the local ladies about 300 to 1 so our chances weren't so hot anyway. But, as my war played out, I didn't have much time to get to know the British women or to learn the local customs.

Chapter 10

Lucifer II

One morning about three weeks after we arrived at Grafton Underwood four new B-17F Flying Fortresses appeared out of the mist shortly after breakfast. This was the day we had been waiting for; one of those planes was destined for us! Lt Williams called us together for a briefing that evening and filled us in on his afternoon conversation with the Squadron Commander. We would familiarize ourselves with our new ship the next day and, after our crew chief spent about 36 hours checking out all the aircraft's systems, we would spend the next week taking practice runs over the English countryside, venturing out over the English channel halfway to France to practice finding our way home – time well spent for a pilot who one day soon might have to nurse an ailing ship back to its base. Finally, if all went well on a simulated mission with a training pilot, we would be cleared to go on the next mission which all the rumors promised would be aimed at a target in Germany.

Using his prerogative as the Aircraft Commander, Lt Williams had decided on the name "Lucifer" for our new plane. He said he chose it because he wanted us to be a helluva nuisance to the Germans. He had designed some art work for the nose but we had to wait in line for the Group's painters to get caught up putting all the Group and Squadron markings on the newly-arrived ships before they could get around to nose art. About that time, the Lieutenant got the word that there already was a B-17 named Lucifer so he had to come up with another name. Being a resourceful fellow, he added the Roman numeral II after the name, stuck with his original nose art, and our ship became "Lucifer II". Things moved quickly after that and it turned out that the Lieutenant's art work – or any other art work - never did get painted on Lucifer II's nose.

Our new Aircraft had rolled out of the Boeing factory in production block B-17F-75-BO with serial number 42-29867 making it an F model. The design had seen a lot of modifications since the prototype's first flight on 28 July 1935 and ours had all the latest updates: larger engines gave better performance and payload, increased fuel capacity gave greater range, and more armament gave better defensive capabilities. I was pleased to find that our ship had the removable covers for the waist gunners' windows just starting to appear on the F models; maybe I would survive the cold blasts after all. The famous *Memphis Belle*, the first B-17 I had ever seen, was also an F model, so I felt pretty good about riding in Lucifer II.

The basic US Army Air Forces philosophy was that each bomber crew member should know all the jobs on the plane for emergencies; each officer was supposed to be capable of manning any of the ship's guns - except for the turrets he couldn't fit into of course. And obviously, that didn't mean us lowly gunners had to know the pilot's, the navigator's, or the bombardier's job or the radio operator's job either, but as a waist gunner I was expected to be an expert on all the on-board guns including those in the turrets. One of my little extra duties as we approached a combat zone was to help the ball-turret gunner insert himself into that ridiculously-exposed position hanging down from the belly of the aircraft. I thanked the luck that made me a little bit too large to fit down into that hell hole. The Army Air Forces thoughtfully provided 30-pound flak suits, steel helmets, and parachutes – the wearing of which made movement all but impossible. Most guys didn't strap all that stuff on, but we wore harnesses that parachutes could snap onto quickly and nobody ever let his chute get too far out of reach. Most of us snapped on the chutes when the shooting started.

After the War I enjoyed reading about the inventions developed for the military at such a rapid pace in the late 1930s and early 1940s. Both sides in WWII had some potent new technologies working for them. The

Germans had new weapons such as the V-2 rocket and the first operational jet fighter, the Messerschmidtt Me 26, and several other advances that never saw the light of day before the war ended. The Allied Forces had radar and sonar and sensational new aircraft such as the F-51 and eventually the atomic bomb. But no high-tech invention was more important in bringing the war to German soil than the top secret Norden Bombsight.

Carl Norden had been developing this device from the 1920s, and by the mid-1930s the US Navy was the first to buy them. As early as 1935 the US Army began to use them as well and started developing the tactics of high-altitude, precision daylight bombing. Norden had planned to produce 800 bombsights in 1941, but Pearl Harbor changed all that and production was sharply increased so that by the end of 1943 his plants were churning out 2,000 a month. The Norden factories closed in 1945 after producing more than 43,000 of the devices. Unlike most of the weapons manufacturers, whose often-expressed patriotism did not prevent them from building in high profit margins on sales to the US Government, Norden did not make any money from his invention; in 1941 he sold the rights to the US government for $1.00.

One of the advantages of finally being combat-ready was that we got our first look at the famous bombsight we had heard so much about. The Norden sights were classified Top Secret. Bombardiers had to sign for them and swear to destroy them before letting them fall into enemy hands. On the ground the devices were kept covered to shield them from prying eyes and they were only unwrapped after takeoff. Just so we would all know what was going on, our bombardier, Lt Tom Breen, briefed our crew on the bombsight's capabilities stressing the high level of security we were all required to maintain. Then Lt Williams took over and reviewed the concept of precision daylight bombing and our role in it. We had heard all this stuff before but only in bits and pieces and it was useful to have it all pulled together, especially now when we would soon be doing it for real.

The whole idea of high-altitude, precision daylight bombing really grew out of the introduction of the Norden Bombsight – which provided a new level of accuracy in delivering bombs on targets. With information the bombardier would enter – like altitude, airspeed, and wind direction – the sight would do the calculations and release the bombs at the optimal moment. In 1935 the Army Air Corps equipped a group of Martin B-10 bombers with the sights and began working out the details. Army fliers reported that, with the Norden Bombsight, they could drop a bomb into a pickle barrel.

The US military took the Top Secret classification of Carl Norden's revolutionary bombsight very seriously. As I said earlier, every effort was made to keep examples from falling into enemy hands; although undocumented to my knowledge, attempts to keep the instrument from the enemy quite likely cost some US fliers their lives. Norden's factories were considered to be among the most security-conscious of all the plants involved in war production, so the sights with treated with the greatest security at every level. But all these efforts were a waste of time; the Germans had had the blueprints for the Norden Bombsight since 1937, thanks to Hermann W. Lang. A 35 year-old German immigrant, Lang worked as an inspector in the Norden plant at 80 Lafayette Street in Manhattan. His position gave him access to the bombsight plans and over a matter of months he gradually smuggled them via Abwehr couriers to Luftwaffe engineers in Germany who constructed their own version of the device before the US had even entered into the war. Lang's spying did not deprive our fliers of the advantages of the bombsight but it gave the enemy the same advantages.

Lang was arrested by the FBI in 1941 through the efforts of the US double-agent William Sebold as part of the famous Duquesne spy ring roundup which netted 33 German agents. They were tried in Federal District Court in Brooklyn and found guilty on 31 December 1941. Hermann Lang served nine years in US prisons; he was deported to his homeland in 1950 where he was largely unemployed for the rest of his life. Whether or not he had been planted by the Germans with the intention of activating him as a spy when the moment was right was never answered. He continued to insist he was never a spy but rather a German patriot. Similar reasoning seems to have been used by many Germans who accepted Hitler as their Supreme Leader and committed unspeakable atrocities in his name and the name of the Third Reich.

A mystery remains, for which I have been unable to find an explanation. Since Hermann Lang was convicted in 1941 of espionage for stealing the plans for the Norden Bombsight, why did the Bombsight remain Top Secret until it was declassified in 1944. Despite requests from the British Government, Bomber Command was not given access to the device until 1943; if they had it sooner would it have changed their attitude toward precision bombing? What effect might that have had on the course of the war? "Security" at the Norden factories was maintained at great expense until 1944. American Air Forces were required to follow extreme measures to guard the Bombsight as our most highly classified device until 1944, at great cost in money and manpower, if not human life. The American public did not learn of Carl Norden's invention until its declassification in 1944. Why did this device, with its blueprints known to be in the hands of the Luftwaffe, remain Top Secret for three more years? Is it possible that the nature of Lang's crime was not brought to the attention of the War Department in 1941? Were the crimes of these convicted spies not publicized during the trial? It seems highly likely that this information was known at the highest levels of the Roosevelt

Administration; was it withheld from the public and our own military forces for some reason? Or were we all so distracted in December of '41 by Pearl Harbor and our entry into the war that the crimes received little attention? Regardless, it seems incredible that the Norden Bombsight remained as one of our most closely guarded secrets until 1944 - although by 1941 we knew it had been comprised. This breakdown in communication, whether intentional or not, seems inexcusable - yet to my knowledge it has never been explained.

By the time WWII began, US leaders were convinced that high-altitude, precision daylight bombing was the superior approach, capable of more effectively targeting military installations and production facilities and promising to be more effective in reducing civilian casualties compared to the British approach of nighttime saturation bombing. Hundreds of US aircraft would fly in tight formation to concentrate massive amounts of firepower against enemy fighters. High-altitude flight paths at levels fighters strained to reach would also provide some defense – or so the American planners thought. To keep the enemy guessing about the target, the formation would change headings several times until reaching the initial point in the bomb run, the IP; at that time the pilot would hand over control of the aircraft to the bombardier and the Norden sight, linked to the autopilot, would take it from there, releasing the bombs at the ideal point in space and time.

The idea was sound but there were some problems that had to be dealt with. For one thing, during heading changes big formations tended to fan out as ships on the outside of the turn, having further to travel, could not keep up with those on the inside. Loose formations made the enemy fighter pilots' life much easier. Another problem was that none of our fighters had the range to accompany the bombers more than half-way to the target and the Germans knew it; their fighters would delay their attack on the formation until our escorts had to turn for home. This dilemma ended with the arrival in England of the F-51 Mustang with its long range - but not until 1944 - and my war was over by then. One of the thorniest problems for the guys actually flying the missions was a feature of the Norden Bombsight itself. From the IP to the target the aircraft had to be held as stable as possible - with no changes of altitude, airspeed, or heading - so the bombsight could do its job. With no evasive maneuvers permitted the bombers were sitting ducks during this time. The last few minutes to the target could test any flyer's courage. It is hard to explain where all the bravery came from, but there it was and the 8th USAAF did more than its share of damage to the German war effort, eventually proving to be a major factor in the outcome of WWII.

The relative merits of precision daylight bombing as favored by the Americans vs. nighttime saturation bombing as favored by the British were a source of contention between the Allies. After finding that the accuracy of its bomb drops was less than 20% in early raids on military and industrial targets, the British Air Ministry decided to concentrate on nighttime saturation bombing of major cities, claiming that this approach would destroy the morale of the German people and ultimately drive them to pressure their government to sue for peace. Before the war began, US planners believed that tight formations of big bombers with their massed firepower could penetrate German defenses even without fighter escorts and that the precision bombing they could achieve with the Norden Bombsight – not yet shared with the British – would carry the day. Moreover, they believed that this approach would bring the war to an end more quickly. The debate over this issue was often bitter and the arguments continue to this day. The war continued for more than three and one-half more years; by V-E day most German cities were essentially leveled and there were almost four million German civilian casualties.

Within days after the Japanese attacked Pearl Harbor both Germany and Italy declared war on the United States. On 22 December 1941 Churchill visited FDR at the White House; they agreed upon a massive buildup of American bombers in England on airfields to be provided by the British. However, the British were not always gracious hosts. Initially, "they cooperated 100% in every respect" in the words of Ira Eakers, but in some respects the cooperation gradually deteriorated. Apart from their persistent criticism of precision bombing, they were highly critical of the B-17 when the aircraft first arrived in England on 1 July 1942.

Air Marshal Arthur "Bomber" Harris, appointed by Churchill a few months earlier as Commander-in-Chief of British Bomber Command, was one of the most outspoken critics of everything American and many of his officers followed his example; he seemed to still harbor some resentment for the fact that George III was unable to repress the colonials. After inspecting one of the first B-17s to arrive in England, RAF officers said its defensive fire power was '"too weak to afford reasonable protection", the tail gun position was "too cramped", and the belly turret was "so awkward as to be useless". Taking his lead from the RAF, critic Peter Masefield, writing in the *London Times,* contended that "American heavy bombers - the latest Fortresses and Liberators - are fine flying machines, but not suited for bombing in Europe. Their bomb loads are small, their armour and armament are not up to the standards now found necessary, and their speeds are low". Harris had nothing but disdain for the American bombing strategy and - consistent with his reputation as the epitome of arrogance - he took every opportunity to express it, including ridiculing the American's choice of targets. So, although the British had given US forces excellent cooperation during the buildup of 1942 and 1943, there were major, on-going philosophical differences between the air arms of the two allies. Unfortunately, I was not consulted on these issues at the time.

Finally the day came when *Lucifer II* showed up on the mission board. We weren't actually expecting it just then; the rumors were we would have to stand down until a sufficient force could be assembled for the second raid on Schweinfurt and it was clear that we weren't ready for that yet. As it turned out our mission never happened. Preparations, complete with the fresh-egg breakfast crews bound for combat were always served but few guys had the appetite for, were nerve-racking to put it mildly. There was plenty of time for our fears to gnaw on our stomachs as we waited in the airplane for more than two hours for the signal to start our engines. The signal never came. The mission was scrubbed due to overcast over the target and an unfavorable weather forecast. So we cleaned the guns anyway and wrapped them up again for storage. Any ideas that we would be counting down from 24 missions by the end of the day were forgotten. At least we had a practice session on dealing with real live fear.

By now the bomber groups were sending up anything that could fly, so when a mission was posted we knew we would be in on it. Sure enough, there we were, listed on the mission board a few days later. Rumor had it this was considered a "milk run" - a relatively easy mission with a good chance of coming home. Again, we sweated through the preparations and the takeoff – always tense in a B-17 fully loaded with fuel and bombs – and then, for the first time, we went through the process of forming up with the other Bomber Groups. With hundreds of planes to be assembled into one huge formation this was obviously a complex deal requiring a lot of circling and waiting and a handful of color-coded lead ships to get everyone in place - and some pretty good flying by a bunch of low-time pilots. Fortunately for the success of the mission, waist gunners were just spectators in this process. We were still trying to settle our nerves as the coast of France came into view when engine #2 suddenly quit. B-17s were quite capable of flying on three engines, or just two for that matter, even fully loaded - if the pilot could feather the prop on the sick engine(s), otherwise the drag would slowly pull the aircraft down. Lt Williams succeeded in quickly feathering #2, but the loss of an engine at that point meant our mission was over and we headed for home. And it did turn out to be a milk run. Everyone came home except for one badly shot-up B-17 ditched smartly in the Channel by another one of those low-time pilots; all of his crewmates came home with him – alive. Meanwhile, everyone in our crew was probably thinking the same thing I was – our second try and still no credit for a mission. Like Alice's Red Queen, we were running as fast as we could just to stay in place.

So we headed for home to sit and bite our nails as we counted the squadron's returning aircraft. As we approached the English coast it was clear that the entire island would soon be socked in; the returning bombers would be hard pressed to locate their home bases. The drill in such cases was to find the nearest US or British airfield and to put those expensive airplanes - and their priceless crews - safely on the ground.

We made it safely home before the worst of the weather descended, but it was several hours later before the Group's other aircraft began straggling in. Word soon trickled down that all but two of our B17s had made it safely back to England. One third of them ended up at other bases but the rest made it home OK.

We also had some stragglers from other US stations in East Anglia who landed at Grafton Underwood seeking the safety of the nearest friendly tarmac. One of those B-17s was the *Grin & Greeter* of the 447th Bombardment Group based at Rattlesden. As their crew disembarked I realized I recognized one of them, a gunner named Hank Corrow. I had run into him a couple of times Stateside and remembered him as a pretty good guy.

The *Grin & Greeter* ended up spending two nights at Grafton Underwood before the heavy blanket of fog lifted from England and, since none of our crews were going anywhere in that weather either, the bar was open. We concentrated on enjoying the respite. The visiting crews were more than welcome to join the revelries; we always needed some new war stories to liven up the party, and Hank Corrow and the other gunners from his crew had plenty of stories.

For some reason, maybe because they occupy the most insane position on a B-17, ball-turret gunners like Hank always seem to take the most ribbing - but they also seem to have the best stories. Hank told of a close call when the flak got so bad the help he needed to get out of the turret arrived in the nick of time; he just got his legs pulled up into the plane when the turret took a direct hit and was blown clean off. He also told the much sadder story of a fellow belly-gunner trapped in the ball as his ship came limping in for an unavoidable gear-up landing with the terrible outcome everyone, including the gunner, knew was inevitable. Hank tried to keep it light saying he had "the best seat in the house" in the *Grin & Greeter*. He described a recent trip when, after recovering from nearly freezing to death, he found the cord powering his electrically-heated suit had come unplugged. He also claimed he had become so comfortable in the ball that he started taking a blanket and pillow down there with him and got lots of sack time coming and going to combat zones. Anyone who had ever peered down into the belly gunner's turret on a B-17 knew Hank was putting us on.

S/Sgt Henry W Corrow (1923 - 1986)

708th Squadron, 447th Bombardment Group

Member, The Greatest Generation

After the war I looked up Hank Corrow and we exchanged a few letters. He survived 29 missions over Germany to wrap up his tour of duty, receiving his "Lucky Bastards" certificate to prove it. The original 25 mission requirement had been increased to 30 but the war ended before he had time for the last one. Hank went home to pursue the career in journalism he had always planned on before the "big interruption" and lived to raise a big family in New Hampshire.

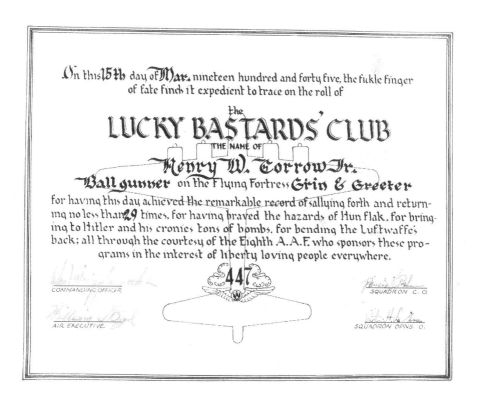

Chapter 11

Black Thursday

On 14 October 1943 the US Eighth Air Force in England launched Mission 115, its second massive raid on the Schweinfurt ball-bearing factories in Germany. The loss of planes and crew members was devastating. Six hundred American fliers were killed or captured that day, a day still known in Air Force lore as "Black Thursday". It altered the American strategy for bombing German targets, and it altered my life.

Ball-bearings were considered one of the most critical industries for the German war effort, and the Schweinfurt factories accounted for half the country's production. Two months earlier, on 17 August 1943, the Eighth launched its first raid on Schweinfurt. The original plan for that raid called for an attack on the Messerschmidt Bf 109 factories near Regensburg, but the plan was altered to make it a dual raid on Regensburg and Schweinfurt, launching a total of 376 B-17s. The first wave anticipated encountering German fighters as it crossed the French coast; the second wave, following the same route across the Channel but bound for Schweinfurt 110 miles to the southeast, hoped to slip through before the Luftwaffe could refuel and regroup.

Not everything went as planned. England awoke to a blanket of fog that morning and the aircrews mounted up and waited for the signal to go. At 0800 the 4th Bomb Wing, constituting the first wave, with its 146 B-17s led by Curtis LeMay and bound for Regensburg, was given clearance to take off. However, the 1st Bomb Wing, with its 230 B-17s led by Robert Williams, assigned to the second wave bound for Schweinfurt, was still grounded by fog. As expected, LeMay's force encountered heavy fighter opposition losing 15 bombers but fought its way through, encountered little flak over the target, and dropped 300 tons of high explosives on the Messerschmidt factories. Nine more aircraft were lost on their route south to US airbases in North Africa, an escape route designed to lead the German fighters away from the incoming second wave of B-17s. But by the time the 1st Bomb Wing was approaching the coast of France, well behind schedule and with a wide gap between the two waves, German fighters had regrouped and attacked 300-strong with devastating effects; 22 B-17s were lost to the fighters and an additional 3 aircraft were lost in the heavy flak over the target. The German fighters were not done with them yet. When the 1st Bomb Wing turned back toward England after delivering its bomb load it was jumped again by the Messerschmidts and lost another 11 B-17s.

The combined Schweinfurt-Regensburg raid started out with 376 B-17s and cost the USAAF 60 bombers and 55 aircrews totaling 552 men. Half the casualties became prisoners of war while 20 were interned by the Swiss. The rest were killed outright. Four Allied fighter pilots were also lost in the battle. In each case their war was over and the pipe-line had to come up with their replacements. Worst of all, 556 telegrams went off to homes all over America. The tactics planned to thwart the German fighters fell victim to the lack of coordination between the two waves of bombers. The inability of mission planners to cover contingencies was beginning to raise the ire of the guys in the trenches. Morale among VIII Bomber Command crews reached new lows.

These losses were shocking and the entire American Air Force in England had to fall back and rebuild in terms of both aircraft and crews. Nevertheless, American planners felt the results of the raid on Schweinfurt were promising and there was every reason to believe a follow-up raid could create a serious interruption in the flow of this critical war element; they were probably right but they didn't follow through quickly enough. The Nazi Armaments Minister, Albert Speer, said after the war that the Americans made a "crucial mistake" in splitting its August 7 force between Regensburg and Schweinfurt; an attack on Schweinfurt alone by the combined 376 bombers of the 1st and 4th Bomb Wings would probably have inflicted enough damage to force the Germans to permanently abandon the ball-bearing plants there with serious consequences for German military efforts. Speer also said that the two-month delay in launching a second attack on the factories gave Germany the time to disperse ball bearing production to several other locations and to prepare their defenses against an anticipated second raid on Schweinfurt.

But the second raid on Schweinfurt had to wait while damaged aircraft were repaired, new aircraft arrived, and new crew members came on board. By 8 October 1943, VIII Bomber Command (it didn't become the 8th Air Force until 22 February 1944) was ready to resume raids on German targets but even then the second raid on Schweinfurt was not their top priority. And the losses continued at an alarming rate. In the days leading up to Schweinfurt II, 88 B-17s were lost in three separate raids on other targets (8, 9 and 10 May). A total of 900 men were lost over those three days.

The morning of 14 October 1943 was cold and wet when we were awakened before dawn. As expected, Lucifer II was on the board again, this time for our third try at completing our first mission. The briefing room was overcrowded, with crew members sitting in the aisles and leaning against the walls as the operations officer pulled back the black drape covering the mission board. All eyes focused on the red target string and a moan went up when we realized it ended at Schweinfurt. The first raid on that city and the price exacted by German defenders was on every mind. The briefer drew another moan, louder than the first, when he suggested, perhaps with a misplaced attempt at humor, that the day's raid might be another milk run.

As the mission's target began to sink in, I must admit I was pretty nervous going through the usual preparations. We needed to get a mission under our belts and get the magic count down to twenty-four. It was a bit strange when you thought about it; all of us had volunteered for combat duty and now that it was here we couldn't wait to start the countdown that would get us home. It wasn't that anything was really worse than we expected; we had known what we were getting into – more or less. And most of us still had that spark of patriotism and desire to meet the enemy and kill as many as possible, although killing was something we were starting to feel differently about as we watched our own guys buy the farm. And now we knew that the Command was facing losses that threatened our ability to stay in the fight and now we knew a lot more about the probability of surviving the whole thing. And now we faced a dead-serious mission deep into Germany and we knew we hadn't been personally tested yet and we didn't know how we would respond. A few days earlier I had a few beers with a senior gunner from another squadron and we got to talking about controlling fear going into combat. He offered a piece of advice that I thought might work for me; he said that I should consider myself dead already and then just go about my business. For some reason that reminded me of something my brother Richie had tried to tell me back in the Golden Gloves experiment: if you worry about the other guy hurting you it's hard to concentrate on hurting him. Sure, you do your best to ward off the incoming blows but you can't let them distract you from your goal. I tried to make myself think that way.

We waited a long time in the aircraft as the weather continued to threaten the mission. Crews were expected to be in their places an hour before the planned take-off time. That meant we were suited up in all the gear we would wear for the day – an electrically-heated outfit under our flying suit, with a leather jacket and a Mae West over that just in case we took a dip in the Channel, plus our bulky, sheepskin-lined flying boots. In the plane we would put on a 30-pound flak jacket and a leather helmet topped off with a tin hat as we approached the combat zone. Even earlier, as we started gaining altitude we would need the oxygen mask, the electrically-heated suit, and the heavy gloves. Believe it or not the temperatures could reach minus 40 degrees F or worse at altitude. Window covers helped a little by cutting down on the 170 mph wind but it was still frigid up there. Sitting on the ramp with all our insulation we were anything but cold despite the chill outside as we waited for the signal to start our engines; in fact, sweat was an enemy we didn't want to carry to the freezing temperatures at 25,000 feet or so, but there wasn't much we could do about it. What did we think about as the hours ticked off? I thought about Mom and Pop and all my siblings back in Yonkers and I figured they'd be sad for a little while but they'd survive if I went down; at least I didn't have a wife and a kid to leave behind. When we climbed aboard the plane at 0700 the visibility was one-quarter mile; by 1000 hours it had lifted to one mile and a recon plane reported clear skies over the continent - the mission was on; the green flare to start our engines finally went up.

The takeoff roll in a fully loaded B-17 was always a nail-biter. That day, with the officially-approved extra ammo for the .50 cal guns we were even heavier than usual. The red lights at the end of the 5,000 ft runway seemed to come closer faster than ever – or so I am told. I couldn't see them from my seat but by then I had a good idea of how long our take-off roll should be and I was relieved to feel that unmistakable sensation of an aircraft responding to the wind under its wings and lifting off Mother Earth. Due to the low visibility the interval between take-off rolls was increased from 30 seconds to 1 min; the increased distance between ships somewhat decreased the wake turbulence each bomber after the first one had to cope with, making the takeoff roll a little easier for the pilot to control. He had enough to handle that day; within a couple of seconds after lifting off, we were totally in the soup, meaning he had to transition from ground references to instruments very quickly – not the easiest thing in the world to do, but there were no accidents on takeoff except for one B-17 that veered off the runway and became mired in the mud; no mission for them that day. So before we even left the station we were starting out one ship short. We continued to climb at 120 mph in the soup for what seemed like hours. The forecast had the tops of the clouds at 2,000 feet but we didn't break out until 6,500 feet. Forming up took longer than usual and we started off across the Channel climbing to 27,000 feet, - way behind schedule.

The 93rd and the 392nd Bomb Groups, flying B-24 Liberators, were assigned to a route to the south of the our flight path and were scheduled to rendezvous with us as we approached the target. However, we learned later that in the thick fog that fatal Thursday morning only 29 of the 60 B-24s scheduled to fly the mission could take off; eight of these were unable to form up in the thick clouds and returned to base. The remaining 21 Liberators made a diversionary sweep toward Emden. Meanwhile, twenty-six B-17s had aborted the mission for various reasons. Of the 351 bombers that set out to hit Schweinfurt, 86 weren't with us. Before the enemy had fired a shot, a variety of screw-ups had reduced our attacking force – and our defensive firepower - by almost 25%. As we flew across France 37 more B-17s fell victim to German fighters, so only 228 bombers of the 351 in the original plan actually made it to Schweinfurt – about 2/3 of the original striking force.

Earlier, as we approached the French coast all eyes were searching for the escort we were told to expect: P-41s, P-38s and Spitfires. Two Groups of P-41s showed up, the 353rd and the 56th; they stuck with us long enough to shoot down 13 German fighters. But we learned later (much later in my case) that the 4th Fighter Group couldn't locate the B-17 formation and aborted; the 352nd Fighter Group went on the diversionary raid with the Liberators. The 55th Fighter Group in P-38s did not become operational until the next day - some planner seems to have overlooked that little detail. The Spitfires, presumably grounded by fog, never appeared at all. All this didn't mean a whole lot to me at the time; all I knew was that the Brass had sent us out expecting a substantial fighter escort that didn't show up due to what surely seemed to be unrealistic, overly optimistic planning. The weather had caused all sorts of screw-ups in the schedule right from the get-go, and there didn't seem to be any contingency plans; nobody seemed to be in charge of the big picture once all the plans were filed. At least that's how it looked to me, way down at the bottom of the totem pole.

The German fighters were obviously well aware of the range limitations of the P-41s; they held off their attacks until our "Little Friends" reached the limits of their fuel range and had to peel off. The action was fast and furious from then on. We had heard intelligence reports that all 1,100 German fighters available in the sector were staged within 85 miles of our flight path, and there was no question that the enemy knew we were coming – they had us on radar before we crossed the English coastline - so we knew we were flying straight into Hell. We faced wave-after-wave of fighter attacks along the 350 or so air miles from the English Channel to the IP. It could only be called a hair-raising first taste of combat for me, with things happening so fast I was acting completely on reflexes.

We had never seen anything like this in all our hours of practice – but how could you simulate it? I tried to maintain the discipline we had been taught – not firing before the target was in range and keeping bursts short to conserve ammo. Several times I thought I could see my tracers stitching up the side of an Me 109 but I never saw any damage from my efforts. We had been told their pilots had the habit of rolling on their backs at crucial moments and pulling into steep dives making it hard to tell if they had taken any hits. I was too busy to worry about it anyway. This went on for more than an hour and a half but as we approached the target the fighters peeled off as the flak picked up; the German pilots didn't want their own flak bringing them down. Somehow, Lucifer II had flown though this gantlet of terror without experiencing any serious damage.

From the IP inbound our Bombardier, Lt Breen, took control of the aircraft and held us steady as we sweated our way toward the target; the Norden Bombsight dropped our thousand-pounders just as planned. We didn't wait around to see where they landed. It was too soon to start relaxing, but I couldn't help but think we finally got that first mission in. Though I was too scared to think about it and too busy to worry about it, I had been able to continue functioning. Had I passed Hemingway's test? Lt Williams took over Lucifer II's controls again and started our sweeping right turn to head for home; the Luftwaffe's fighters were back overhead immediately. Just then a rocket – fired from a twin-engine fighter standing off beyond the range of our guns - hit engine 2, knocking it out completely. Our stalwart pilots fought to feather the prop, hitting the feathering button, the ignition switch, the fuel-cutoff switch and chopping the throttle. It worked; a feathered prop turns a knife-edge into the wind, stops turning and offers very little drag compared to a windmilling prop. Advancing the throttles on our remaining engines, the pilots hoped we could keep up with the formation.

Fighters were all over us again on the way out from the target and this time we were not so lucky. Flying on 3 engines, we were able to keep up with the other B-17s in the formation for a while until they started to climb but then we didn't have the power to stay with them. We felt pretty lonely all by ourselves up there as we started to slip behind the formation – a straggler – just what the enemy fighters pilots wanted. Before long, engine 4 took a hit, caught fire and this time the prop could not be feathered. The drag of that spinning disc, added to the fact that we were now down to 2 engines, meant we were going down. Our radio operator kept sending SOS signals trying to call in some friendly fighters to escort us but we were beyond their range; he wasn't worried about giving away our position – enemy fighters were all over us already. We were lucky in one respect: although we had lost two engines, the airplane had not suffered any other serious damage and nobody had been injured, Once again, our crew came through. Lt Abele pinpointed our position as about 40 miles east of Metz, France – definitely German territory. Lt Williams and our copilot, Lt Candler, were so cool you might have thought they had been doing this all their lives – grace under the ultimate pressure. We got lucky again when the Me 109 pilot must have figured we were done for, trailing flames and smoke and heading down at a pretty good clip. He took off looking for another straggler I guess; sorry I never had the chance to thank him.

After the war I came across a quotation in *Aviation History Magazine* from Lt Carl Abele who mentioned the fact there had never been time to paint the name "Lucifer II" on our plane during the couple of busy weeks it was assigned to us. He went on to summarize our day nicely:

"The Fighters were unrelenting; it was simply murder,' recalls Carl Abele, who was serving as navigator on a 544th Squadron, 384th Bomb Group B-17F, the Lucifer II.

"As it turned out, the name was destined never to be painted on" Abele remembers. "We lost an engine to flak and another to fighters, but the prop on one of the engines couldn't be feathered. The drag of the dead engine was tremendous, and helped doom the plane. Our pilot held her steady while we all bailed out, then he came out last. I never saw my chute open. The next thing I knew 1 was lying down in the back of a "Totenkopf" (Death's Head) SS Army Division truck on the way to POW camp."

I do remember my chute opening and looking up wondering "What's a nice kid from Yonkers doing in a spot like this?" I didn't have long to muse over it, but I do remember thinking – although I knew the odds perfectly well – until then I had been sure this was never going to happen to me. We were pretty low by the time we bailed out. One of the casualty reports said Lt Williams was down to 500 feet when he left the dying bird. I don't know our altitude when I jumped but one of the reports said we were at about 2,000 feet at that point. The pilots had been stretching our glide as far as they could, thinking we were at least getting further away from the German border. When the order to bail out came we didn't stand around thinking about it but we were out the door in a hurry. I guess I pulled the ripcord as soon as I was clear of the plane; at least, that's what I had been taught to do. We never did a real jump from a plane in training. I think there was a fine line between sending guys off ready to cope with whatever happened or scaring them half to death before they got out of training. We did spend some time learning how to handle our chutes and how to land, first from a two foot-high platform and then from one six feet high: "Feet together and knees flexed – land and roll" was our instructor's war cry. Then we had one jump off a high tower where we fell free for maybe 15 feet or so until our harness caught up with a cable that stopped us with a jerk and we slid down the cable to the ground. It had all been calibrated to simulate the real thing as much as possible, I suppose. And, to tell the truth, everything the instructor had never stopped yelling about came back to me in those few moments over France. I never had time to realize how scared I was. My landing in a hay field was pretty soft. It turned out landing was the least of my problems.

I was pretty sure all the members of our crew had been able to get out of the plane. The officers had been heroes as far as I was concerned; before the command to bail out they stayed cool and made sure all of us had our chutes on, had the few things we needed to take along, and knew which door to head for. We were out of ammo for the .50 cal guns at this point and I headed for the door on the starboard side in the rear of the fuselage after I helped the belly gunner up out of the ball-turret. The co-pilot, Lt Candler, actually gave the order to jump at the command of Lt Williams whose microphone had been shot away by 20 mm fire. Lt Williams made sure everyone else got out and he was the last one to jump.

Years later, as I tried to gather all the facts I could come up with about Mission 115 to Schweinfurt, the USAF provided me with all the information I asked for and more. Some of these documents, including the Missing Air Crew Report and several of the Crew Casualty Questionnaires, are shown in these pages. I tried to learn what had become of all the other members of the crew of Lucifer II in its short war. The happiest news was that everyone had bailed out safely and eventually made it home – in various stages of repair. The real point is that, on our one and only mission, we dropped our bombs on the target and, even though it took a while – the better part of two years in my case - we all came home from that trip into Hell. I would claim that made the mission of Lucifer II to Schweinfurt on Black Thursday a success; Lt Williams should have been awarded a DFC but I guess the Brass was too busy planning their next fiasco.

It turned out that Lt Abele had been seriously injured when he jumped: a broken back, a broken foot and facial injuries. Several of the casualty reports from other members of our crew said they saw him being lifted into a truck, helped by Lt Williams. He was taken to a German Hospital in Metz, then to a POW camp and later, on 5 January 1945, he was shipped back to the US in exchange for a seriously injured German prisoner. He was the only crew member to suffer serious injuries, but he eventually recovered.

VIII Bomber Command continued to take unsustainable losses as summer moved to fall in 1943. Just during the two raids on Schweinfurt, plus the three raids on 8, 9 and 10 October, over 2,000 American lives were lost. It became clear that massive bomber formations with all their defensive firepower could not succeed without fighter escorts. Everyone knew the F-51s were in the pipeline and that they would make a major difference – which proved to be true - but their arrival date was pushed back several times for unexplained reasons. Decisions were made at high levels, and the US reluctantly backed away from the policy of precision daylight bombing of strategic targets as their sole approach. Saturation bombing of major cities became the rule for the majority of mission plans from Black Thursday on. The Allies became hell-bent on reducing Germany to a rubble with no real concern for civilian casualties. The debates still continue as to whether this decision shortened or lengthened the war but there is no question it laid waste to Germany and killed a lot of people.

But back to my visit to France. Suddenly all those lectures about what to do if shot down – yeah, the ones I mostly slept through – seemed a lot more important. The prime lesson had been to avoid capture and head for the American lines. I had a problem right away since there was the little matter of most of France and the English Channel between me and the nearest American lines. An alternative was to seek asylum in Switzerland but first you had to get there. I was still wondering what to do when several people approached; brilliantly I concluded they must be speaking French – which I neither spoke nor understood - so they must be French people. I had concluded earlier that if I was ever shot down in France I would try to link up with the French Resistance and I remember thinking maybe these people would help with such a connection. They seemed friendly enough; they brought me into the farm house, sat me down at the kitchen table, and offered me an apple which I started munching on right away. I had no idea when I had last eaten but just then it seemed a lifetime ago. Ironically, Al Wickline, a fellow crew member I had known since gunnery school days at Kingman, said in his Casualty Questionnaire (Page 125) that he had seen me being escorted into a farm house by two men and a woman and that I looked OK. Neither Al nor I realized my new French friends had sent someone off to tell the Germans they had "caught one", but suddenly a truck full of troops swarmed over the farm house and I was captured before I knew what was happening. The soldiers roughed me up a little "helping" me into the truck, but nothing too bad.

The next few weeks were a blur. I remember being hauled in a truck with 6 or 8 other downed American fliers. One guy reminded us that it was our responsibility to try to escape, but so far I hadn't seen any opportunities for that. I remember at one point being told I would be interrogated but it turned out to be more like a casual interview with a young German officer speaking excellent English. He offered me a cigarette but I refused; we had been told they would try to soften us up and I figured I'd better act tough. He asked me a bunch of the usual questions about the unit I was assigned to and its strength, the morale at our station, the next target we planned to attack and so on but all I answered with was my name, rank and serial number. Finally he told me he didn't really expect me to answer his questions and it really didn't matter; they probably knew more about all that stuff than I did anyway. He was really quite pleasant and told me what would happen to me over the next few days. I learned I would be assigned to a prisoner of war camp for NCOs. I would not have to do manual labor and I could expect to be treated decently. Unfortunately, he didn't know the whole story but at least it wasn't much of an "interrogation". I found it disappointing that I really didn't want to kill the first Kraut I met face-to-face.

If you didn't know Germans were so good at planning things, you might have thought they didn't know what to do with us next. We were moved constantly in trucks and railroad cars and always with a different group of guys - to discourage any escape plots from having a chance to develop, I suppose. Suffice it to say, our comfort was not a high priority with our captors. There was never any heat and we were never supplied with a blanket. Food was in short supply too, and we only had access to water now and then. It was impossible to tell if we were being moved in any particular direction, but rumors were circulating on the grape-vine about a rapidly-expanding camp for NCO flyers a few hundred miles west in Austria, and some of the POWs thought we were headed there. It was called Stalag 17.

The official (declassified) report of Lucifer II's fatal mission, the crew list and other documents provided by the USAF Office of Historical Studies are reproduced on the following pages.

CONFIDENTIAL

WAR DEPARTMENT
HEADQUARTERS ARMY AIR FORCES
WASHINGTON

MISSING AIR CREW REPORT

RESTRICTED

Classification changed
to: CONFIDENTIAL

OK.

IMPORTANT: This report will be compiled in triplicate by each Army Air
Forces organization within 48 hours of the time an aircraft is
officially reported missing.

1. ORGANIZATION: Location AAF Station 106 ; Command or Air Force VIII
   Group 384th ; Squadron 544th ; Detachment

2. SPECIFY: POINT of Departure AAF Station 106 ; Course As Briefed
   Intended Destination Schweinfurt, Germany ; Type of Mission Combat

3. WEATHER CONDITIONS AND VISIBILITY AT TIME OF CRASH OR WHEN LAST REPORTED:
   Cavu over target, but haze and low cloud coverage coming west.

4. GIVE: (a) Date 14 Oct 43 Time Between 1145 & 1545 and Location Between Schweinfurt & Sois
   of last known whereabouts of missing aircraft.
   (b) Specify whether ( ) Last Sighted; ( ) Last contacted by Radio;
   ( ) Forces Down; ( ) Seen to Crash; or ( ) Information not Available.

5. AIRCRAFT WAS LOST, OR IS BELIEVED TO HAVE BEEN LOST, AS A RESULT OF: (Check only
   one ( ) Enemy Aircraft; ( ) Enemy Anti-Aircraft; (x) Other Circumstances as
   follows Lost from formation after attacking target. Under E/A attack, believed shot
   down in Germany

6. AIRCRAFT: Type, Model and Series B-17F; A.A.F. Serial Number 42-29867

7. ENGINES: Type, Model and Series ; A.A.F. Serial Number (a) 42-137567
   (b) 43-56960 ; (c) 42-79420 (d) 42-13749

8. INSTALLED WEAPONS (Furnish below Make, Type and Serial Number)
   (a) ; (b) ; (c) ; (d)
   (e) ; (f) ; (g) ; (h)

9. THE PERSONS LISTED BELOW WERE REPORTED AS: (a) Battle Casualty X
   or (b) Non-Battle Casualty

10. NUMBER OF PERSONS ABOARD AIRCRAFT: Crew 10 ; Passengers ; Total 10
    (Starting with pilot, furnish the following particulars: If more than 10
    persons were aboard aircraft, list similar particulars on separate sheet
    and attach original to this form).

	Crew Position	Name in Full (Last Name First)	Rank	Serial Number
EVS 1. Pilot	Pilot	Williams, Walter Gordon	2nd Lt	O-795863
EVS 2.	Co-Pilot	Candler, Belford Bruce	2nd Lt	O-798066
RMS 3.	Navigator	Abele, Carl William	2nd Lt	O-735151
EVS 4.	Bombardier	Brean, Thomas Carroll, Jr.	2nd Lt	O-676345
EVS 5.	Radio Operator	Hanrahan, Thomas Patrick	T/Sgt	32383135
EVS 8.	Top Turret	Bush, Clyde Thomas	T/Sgt	37128669
EVS 9.	Ball Turret	Genseite, William Reymond	Sgt	16014308
RTD 8.	Tail Gunner	Wickline, Albert John	S/Sgt	15328521
EVS 9.	Right Flexible Gun	Henneberry, Michael Raymond	S/Sgt	32405532
EVS 10.	Left Flexible Gun	Deese, James William	S/Sgt	14139217

11. IDENTIFY BELOW THOSE PERSONS WHO ARE BELIEVED TO HAVE LAST KNOWLEDGE OF AIR-
    CRAFT, AND CHECK APPROPRIATE COLUMN TO INDICATE BASIS FOR SAME:

Name in Full (Last Name First)	Rank	Serial Number	Contacted by Radio	Last Sighted	Saw Crash	Saw Forced Landing
1.						
2.						
3.						

12. IF PERSONNEL ARE BELIEVED TO HAVE SURVIVED, ANSWER YES TO ONE OF THE FOLLOWING
    STATEMENTS: (a) Parachutes were used ; (b) Persons were seen walking away
    from scene of crash ; or (c) Any other reason (Specify) Unknown

13. ATTACH AERIAL PHOTOGRAPH, MAP, CHART, OR SKETCH, SHOWING APPROXIMATE LOCATION
    WHERE AIRCRAFT WAS LAST SEEN.

14. ATTACH EYEWITNESS DESCRIPTION OF CRASH, FORCED LANDING, OR OTHER CIRCUMSTANCES
    PERTAINING TO MISSING AIRCRAFT.

15. ATTACH A DESCRIPTION OF THE EXTENT OF SEARCH, IF ANY, AND GIVE NAME, RANK AND
    SERIAL NUMBER OF OFFICER IN CHARGE HERE

Date of Report 15 October 1943

(Signature of Preparing Officer)
C. H. CROWE, JR.,
Captain, Air Corps,
Adjutant.

CONFIDENTIAL

The Missing Crew Report

AFPPA-12.

CASUALTY QUESTIONNAIRE

1. Your name **ALBERT J. WICKLINE** Rank **S/SGT.** Serial No. **15322854**

2. Organization **394 BomB Gp.** Gp Commander **Julius K. Lacey** Rank **Col.** Sqn CO **Gilmore** Rank **Maj.**
   (full name)   (full name)

3. What year **1943** month **October** day **14** did you go down?

4. What was the mission, **Schweinfurt**, target, **Ball Bearing Fact.** target time, **UNKNOWN**, altitude, **24,000 FT.**, route scheduled, **UNKNOWN**, route flown **UNKNOWN**

5. Where were you when you left formation? **UNKNOWN**

6. Did you bail out? **YES**

7. Did other members of crew bail out? **YES**

8. Tell all you know about when, where, how each person in your aircraft for whom no individual questionnaire is attached bailed out. A crew list is attached. Please give facts. If you don't know, say: "No Knowledge". **EVERYONE BAILED OUT AT SHORT INTERVALS STARTING TO JUMP AT APPROXIMATELY 2,000 FT.**

9. Where did your aircraft strike the ground? **10-15 MILES FROM METZ**

10. What members of your crew were in the aircraft when it struck the ground? (Should cross check with 8 above and individual questionnaires) **NONE**

11. Where were they in aircraft? ————

12. What was their condition? ————

13. When, where, and in what condition did you last see any members not already described above? **S/SGT HENNEBERRY LAST SEEN GOING INTO A FARM HOUSE WITH A WOMAN & TWO MEN. LOOKED O.K.**

14. Please give any similar information on personnel of any other crew of which you have knowledge. Indicate source of information. **SOME OF THE FRENCH PEOPLE TOLD ME THAT ALL OF THE CREW WAS CAPTURED & TAKEN PRISONERS & THAT SOME OF THEM HAD BEEN HURT & WOUNDED.**

(Any additional information may be written on the back)

6-3862, AF

Al Wickline reports seeing Uncle Mike enter French farmhouse.

APPA-11

INDIVIDUAL CASUALTY QUESTIONNAIRE

Name of crew member: A B E L E, Carl William
Rank: 2nd Lt.
Serial number:
Position: Crew (Bomber) or Navigator

Did he bail out? _YES_

Where? _NEAR METZ, FRANCE_

If not, why not? _____

Last contact or conversation just prior to or at time of loss of plane: _SEEN AS_
HE WAS LEAVING PLANE

Was he injured? _YES_

Where was he when last seen? _HOSPITAL IN METZ FRANCE_

Any hearsay information: _BACK BROKEN AND IN CAST FOR QUITE_
SOME TIME - LEG OR ANKLE BROKEN - BAD CUTS
ON FACE

Source: _Co Plt - 2nd Lt B.B. CANDLER_

Any explanation of his fate based in part or wholly on supposition: _I ATTENDED_
HIM WHEN WE WERE FIRST CAPTURED AND KNOW
THAT HE WAS SEVERLY INJURED

Total number of missions of above crew member: _5 (FIVE)_

Dates and destinations if possible: _____

6-5861, AF

Lt Candler's casualty report on Lt Abele

CASUALTY QUESTIONNAIRE

1. Your name ___Thomas C. Breen Jr.___ Rank _1st Lt_ Serial No. _O-676345_

2. Organization _384_ Gp Commander ___Lacey___ Rank _Col_ Sqn CO __Gilmore__ Rank _Major_
   (full name)   (full name)

3. What year ___1943___ month ___October___ day _14_ did you go down?

4. What was the mission, _Schweinfurt_, target, _Ball-bearing facto,_ target
   time, _14:30_ ,altitude, _22,500_ route scheduled, _In thru_
   Holland,out thru ,route flown _same_
   France

5. Where were you when you left formation? _Over Lorraine, France_

6. Did you bail out? ___Yes___

7. Did other members of crew bail out? __Yes, all.__

8. Tell all you know about when, where, how each person in your aircraft for whom no
   individual questionnaire is attached bailed out. A crew list is attached. Please
   give facts. If you don't know, say: "No Knowledge". Lt. W.G.Williams,pilot,
   bailed out last from about 500 feet.Lt,B.B.Candler,copilot, bailed out
   thru bomb bay.S/Sgt. Gillette bailed out just before the pilot.No
   knowledge on how other crew members bailed out

9. Where did your aircraft strike the ground? _About 5 miles from Metz, France_

10. What members of your crew were in the aircraft when it struck the ground? (Should
    cross check with 8 above and individual questionnaires) _None_

11. Where were they in aircraft? _____

12. What was their condition? _____

13. When, where, and in what condition did you last see any members not already des-
    cribed above? Last saw members not included above except Sgt. Wickline,
    tail gunner, in LeHavre, France, May 1945.

14. Please give any similar information on personnel of any other crew of which you
    have knowledge. Indicate source of information. _____

(Any additional information may be written on the back)

6-3862,AF

Lt Breen's report on crew members he saw bail out.

CASUALTY QUESTIONNAIRE

1. Your name __Belford B. Candler__ Rank __2nd Lt.__ Serial No. __O-798966__

2. Organization __384__ Gp Commander __Lacy__ Rank __Col.__ Sqn CO __Gilmore__ Rank __Major__
   (full name)   (full name)

3. What year __1943__ month __October__ day __14__ did you go down?

4. What was the mission, __Schweinfurt__ ,target, _____ ,target
   time, _____ ,altitude, _____ route scheduled, _____
   _____ ,route flown _____

5. Where were you when you left formation? __Shortly after leaving the target__

6. Did you bail out? __Yes__

7. Did other members of crew bail out? __The entire crew bailed out.__

8. Tell all you know about when, where, how each person in your aircraft for whom no
   individual questionnaire is attached bailed out. A crew list is attached. Please
   give facts. If you don't know, say: "No Knowledge". __The entire crew__
   __bailed out within about three minutes time of each other near__
   __Metz, France__

9. Where did your aircraft strike the ground? __Near Metz, France__

10. What members of your crew were in the aircraft when it struck the ground? (Should
    cross check with 8 above and individual questionnaires) __None__

11. Where were they in aircraft? _____

12. What was their condition? _____

13. When, where, and in what condition did you last see any members not already des-
    cribed above? __I last saw Lt. C.W. Abele on Jan.5, 1945 when he__
    __left Stalag Luft 3 for repatriation. The rest of the crew I__
    __saw at Camp Lucky Sttike, France on May 16,1945. All were in__
    __good condition.__

14. Please give any similar information on personnel of any other crew of which you
    have knowledge. Indicate source of information. _____

(Any additional information may be written on the back)

6-3862,AF

Lt Candler reports that the entire crew bailed out near Metz, France

2nd Lt. Walter G. Williams	Mrs. Myrtle J. Williams, (mother) Wykoff, Minnesota.
2nd Lt. Belford B. Candler	Mrs. Blanche T. Royal, (mother) 614 Pear, Vineland, New Jersey.
2nd Lt. Carl W. Abele	Mrs. Nonda Marie Abele, (wife) 2325 Riverside Drive, Lakewood, Ohio.
2nd Lt. Thomas C. Breen, Jr.	Mr. Thomas C. Breen, Sr., (father) 30 Cedar Drive, Great Neck, New York.
T/Sgt. Thomas P. Hanrahan	Mr. Francis J. Hanrahan, (brother) 4429 North 18th Street, Philadelphia, Pennsylvania.
T/Sgt. Clyde T. Bush	Mr. Raymond J. Bush, (father) Belle Fourche, South Dakota.
S/Sgt. Michael E. Henneberry	Mrs. Richard Henneberry, (mother) 3 - 5 Park Avenue, Mount Vernon, New York.
S/Sgt. James W. Dease	Mrs. Martha R. Dease, (wife) 236 Second Street, Macon, Georgia.
Sgt. William R. Ganotte	Mrs. Irene Emily Ganotte, (mother) 2415 Whitney, Detroit, Michigan.
Sgt. Albert J. Wickline	Mrs. Mary W. Wickline, (mother) Rural Delivery #3, Pidgeon Road, Salem, Ohio.

Lucifer II crew list with home addresses and next-of-kin.

Chapter 12

Stalag 17B

Most guys who have spent any time as prisoners of war have little, if anything, to say about their experience and I am no exception. I'm sure the psychologists have all kinds of explanations for this, most of them involving the mind's subconscious suppression of unpleasant events. In my case it doesn't seem that complicated; I just don't like to think about stuff that takes me back to my 557 days as a POW. You can call it suppression if you want to, but it is not subconscious. I still have memories from that time, but the most unpleasant ones don't pop into my head much anymore.

I suppose for me the worst aspect of being captured by the enemy was the loss of personal freedom and everything that went with it. I had been a soldier for more than six years when I was captured so I was used to a life of rules and regulations but life in the prison camp made the soldier's life look like fun and games.

For one thing, prisoners were out of the war for the duration, so we wouldn't get to influence the outcome the way most of us had planned and that was a major frustration – especially as we had to deal with some pretty nasty examples of the enemy every day. The uncertainty of how long the war – and our imprisonment – would last was on every prisoner's mind constantly. And what if Nazi Germany won the war? Would we be prisoners forever or would we be shot the next day?

The lack of food was another very unpleasant aspect of life as a POW and it got worse and worse until it got to the point where it couldn't get any worse. Ironically, the more effective the Allies were at destroying the German economy the less able the country was to produce food for its own people, and that had a direct effect on us. As the end of the war approached, food production and distribution had nearly ground to a halt and there was damn little to be wasted on prisoners. The daily meal, almost always the same, consisted of a thin soup with bugs in it, black bread, potatoes and maybe rutabagas. After a while we got used to the bugs in the soup and ate them for nourishment.

Although the food shortage among prisoners has been glossed over in official reports, it was very real and in many cases led to malnutrition and diseases which often had serious, long-term consequences. As the war continued, the daily ration of bread was reduced and the bread contained more and more straw. Potatoes were also a staple of the diet in Stalag 17 but as the war went on and they became harder to get they were replaced to some extent by an increase in chickling peas, sometimes called chick peas or grass peas. It turned out that these legumes are known to cause a serious neurological disorder called lathyrism. This disease has been known since the time of Hippocrates and has been described in humans and animals throughout Europe for centuries. Chickling peas (*Lathyris sativus*) have been implicated as the cause since the 19th Century but it was a difficult disease to understand until it became clear that chickling peas only began to cause illness when they exceeded a certain percentage – about 50% or so - of the daily caloric intake.

German officials undoubtedly knew of this problem – lathyrism in animals and humans due to an excess of chickling peas in the diet was widely understood in Europe. They may have attempted to supplement the POW's diet with a limited quantity of chickling peas, gambling that the limit in daily caloric intake would not be exceeded. This is cutting things a little too close it seems since a given prisoner might decide to eat nothing but the chick peas and the bread and thus be in danger. There were numerous cases in the camp of prisoners suffering from muscle spasticity and weakness in the legs, early symptoms of lathyrism. But lathyrism was never officially diagnosed in Stalag 17 so maybe the Germans succeeded in the gamble if they did take it. Of course, American physicians, having never seen this disease, would be very unlikely to reach a correct diagnosis of lathyrism in a returning POW so we will never know if it affected prisoners of Stalag 17B. But lathyrism aside, the meager diet we had to survive on, some of us for many months and even years, was enough to cause serious long-term health effects. Most of us lost significant amounts of weight during our POW days and malnutrition was common; in fact "emaciated" wasn't too strong an adjective to describe most liberated American POWs. Permanent physical damage followed many of us home. Still speaking of food, the Red Cross packages were welcome sights and I think some of us would not have made it without them. They usually contained some food; cigarettes; a chocolate bar; soap and toothpaste. If all the packages the Red Cross shipped had reached the POWs they would have taken care of a lot of problems. Unfortunately, they arrived erratically and in some cases were confiscated by the guards. When packages did arrive, the Commandant sometimes held them back from the prisoners and on at least one occasion he diverted a major shipment to another site where pilfering was later documented. Even when the packages reached the prisoners, the Germans shut off the regular supply of rations for that day - so nobody got fat on any extra calories.

Water was in very short supply in Stalag 17B. The water taps were only in operation a few hours a day. There was no hot water. The latrines were poorly maintained and had a strong, sickening odor since there always seemed to be a shortage of lime for decontamination. The odor got even worse when the prisoners burned the toilet covers for firewood. The rest of the camp wasn't much to write home about. The barracks we occupied, building 34a, was designed to hold 240 prisoners but by the time I had been there six months we had 400 men under our roof. Each prisoner was assigned to one of the triple-decker bunks with a thin straw mattress. Trying to keep our beds bug-free was a full-time job.

Home, Sweet Home

Stalag 17 was in the village of Gniexendorf, about 4 miles NW of the city of Krems an der Donau (on the Danube), about 38 miles WNW of Vienna. The weather was quite pleasant in the summer but cold the rest of the year and snowy in winter. I never did have any insulating fat and I hated the cold as much as anyone did. I don't think I have ever completely warmed up since my vacation in Austria. There was a stove in each barracks but coal for the stoves was tightly rationed so in the coldest weather we never had enough heat. Any wood that could be pried loose ended up in the stove. When we arrived in the camp the guards issued two thin cotton blankets to each man; the prisoners referred to them as tablecloths. At one point shortly after I arrived the Red Cross issued wool army blankets. I had one for a while but that didn't last long. One day the Commandant sent in trucks to carry away most of our few possessions as we were held in formation on the parade field.

The Red Cross also provided whatever we had for recreation like softball equipment and also supplied items such as books, records and a few musical instruments. The records were important to me since many of them were from the Big Band era. Our chief scrounger came up with an old record player, probably by trading cigarettes with one of the guards; we gave up asking how he got stuff. A couple of guys who were B-17 radio operators a few months earlier had figured out how to tap into the Camp's PA system and they organized our own "radio station". I put together a Big Band show which went "on the air" a couple of times a week using some of the records the Red Cross sent. I filled in some air time with a few of my Hollywood star impressions and sometimes I'd have another prisoner as a guest to talk about the bands and their music. The station also broadcast news bulletins on the progress of the war. One of the prisoners had an AM radio he had fabricated from scratch and he could sometimes pick up friendly news broadcasts. The identity of the radio's owner was a deep secret. The Germans hated the fact that we had access to news, especially as the Allies advanced, but they couldn't find the radio; only a few of his fellow prisoners knew who the owner was – not everyone could be trusted and every now and then a prisoner would be caught spying for our captors, something he lived to regret. Our radio station drove the Commandant crazy; his guards couldn't figure out where our "broadcast" was coming from or how we tapped in and he couldn't afford to shut down the PA system.

A few words about our treatment by the Germans are in order. The Camp Commandant, Oberst Kuhn, was not a nice man. At times he was brutal, other times just cruel. Once one of the prisoners lost it and ran toward the perimeter fence; the Commandant personally ordered him gunned down. Another time a few prisoners escaped but were caught within hours; he ordered them shot in front of all the other prisoners and left their bodies hanging on the fence until the next day. Kuhn was an Army man, unfortunately for us; the rumors said Luftwaffe officers in similar positions treated American fliers better than their Army counterparts. A few of the guards followed Oberst Kuhn's example and there were some injuries from beatings with gun butts and clubs, but most of the guards were not too bad. Most of them were old and didn't like being in the Army at all much less being charged with holding other men prisoner. I think most of us got through the ordeal without any real physical abuse; it was the starvation, the cold, and most of all the captivity itself that wore us down.

Mail call was usually the high point of the day, although for most of the guys most of the time it just meant disappointment. Newly arrived prisoners seldom received any mail for their first six months in the camp and many men were there a year without receiving any. For some reason, incoming and outgoing mail was processed through Stalag Luft 3 near Berlin, and delays were routinely a matter of months. Rumor had it that many letters, coming or going, never made it to their destinations. I wrote occasional letters on the forms the guards provided but we knew they went to a central censorship office and many of them never went any further. After the war I learned that none of my letters made it home. I was in Stalag 17 for almost 19 months and never received any mail – for a very good reason: my parents and everyone else at home thought I was dead. After the initial "missing in action" telegram they received no more information until the war was over. It turned out that the Germans had never registered me as a prisoner with the Red Cross as the Geneva Convention required them to do for all POWs. To the outside world I didn't exist from 14 October 1943 to 6 May 1945. Of course I didn't know that and for quite a while I kept expecting a letter from home. The Germans failed to register a lot of prisoners for unknown reasons; maybe they were try to keep the overcrowding a secret. There were about 4,400 American prisoners in Stalag 17B by the time I arrived and it stayed that way until the war's end – and that was just the American sector of the Camp.

I said earlier that boredom was one of the worst aspects of captivity as a POW, and we tried lots of ways of combating it. There were always escape plans being kicked around, but they were always, except once, doomed to failure and that one time was before my arrival. After I was in the camp about four months I became involved in an attempt to dig a tunnel from an adjacent barracks to the far side of the fences but it didn't get very far. Our captors may have been cruel but they weren't stupid. The tunnel was discovered, but at least we didn't get caught. So we stuck to playing cards and reading the few books in the primitive library and trying like hell to bamboozle the guards with stuff like our radio broadcasts. We had a major distraction just before Christmas in 1944 when two of our fellow

Kregies (short for the German *kriegsgefangenen*, or prisoner of war), Donald Bevan and Edmund Trzcinski decided to write a play the troops could put on just for entertainment. They didn't realize what they were starting; "Stalag 17" was a big hit when a bunch of POWs presented it in our Camp, a bigger hit as a Broadway play after the war, and an even bigger hit as a movie starring William Holden in the early 50s. It didn't stop there as a long-running comedy on American TV was based on the Stalag 17 play; it was called "Hogan's Heros" - you may have heard of it. I played a minor, behind-the-scenes role as a sound-effects man in the Camp production. Several of the friendlier guards couldn't help laughing pretty hard along with us and we all had a lot of fun – despite the circumstances. Leave it to Americans to find humor in something so grim as the lives of POWs. Interestingly, the movie's producers doubted that American movie-goers would have any interest in so serious a topic as life in a prison camp, and so they withheld release of the film for over a year. They must have been a little red in the face when Holden won the best male actor Academy Award for his memorable performance as a prisoner of questionable character in the famous Stalag 17 movie.

By the time April of 1945 arrived in the Krems Valley the inmates of Stalag 17B were very aware that something was up. Our secret radio bulletins reported regularly on Allied advances and we were becoming more and more optimistic about the outcome and starting to hope it might happen soon. By then we were a pretty sorry lot, and it took a major effort to generate any enthusiasm. Many more months under these conditions and we would start dropping like flies. About the first of April American bombers began passing overhead every day, and at night we could see the flashes of bombs landing in the distance.

On 8 April 1945 we awoke to a big surprise: we were ordered to pack up our meager belongings and the gates of the American compound were thrown open. About 4,000 starving and grungy US fliers were herded off on a forced march. Another 900 – considered too sick to make the march – were left behind in the camp; probably half of the rest of us were also too sick to make the march but once those gates opened nobody who could put one foot in front of the other was staying behind. We were divided into groups of about 500 men and an American was made leader of each group. We were still guarded by armed Germans but it looked like many of the guards had taken off, figuring the war was as good as over. The smart ones shed their military uniforms and started trying to pass for local farmers.

We all got Red Cross packages when we started out on the march but they only lasted about a week; after that we got some soup and bread from the Germans once in a while and we were free to scrounge or barter for whatever we could from the locals. We were not interested in trying to escape at that point. We were all convinced that liberation was only a few days away and it was safer to wait it out than to give some guard an excuse to gun us down. Some guys were in fair shape when we started out but by the half-way point we were all just shuffling along as best we could. To say it was a grueling trip doesn't really do it justice but the misery was at least partly offset by the sense of elation that the war was almost over and there was no question who had won. The winter of 1945 had been a very cold one in the Krems Valley and even though it was April the days were still in the 50s and the nights a lot colder; it wasn't bad weather for a long hike but it wasn't so great trying to stay warm at night. Under different circumstances it could have been a scenic walk with the Danube often in view to our left. The Germans were marching us to the northwest, toward the advancing American armies; the rumors were the Krauts thought they would get a better deal surrendering to US troops than to the Russians who were closing in fast and were reportedly within 30 miles of Stalag 17B when we left. It turned out we marched 281 miles over 18 days, ending up at an old Russian prison camp near Branau where we got some more Red Cross packages and tried to put together make-shift shelters.

Suddenly liberation was at hand. On 3 May 1945 three Jeeps drove into the Branau camp carrying six men from the 13th Armored Division. The German guards were down to about 200 at that point and they were not in the mood to put up any fight. We were free. A memory from the day we were shot down flashed into my mind; the nearest US lines were so far away that day but by a very long and circuitous route, here I was safely behind them again.

When we were liberated I think we were all numb. We were miserable specimens physically and mentally and really didn't know how to react. Those of us who had been in captivity the longest seemed to have the hardest time adjusting to the new reality: we were free - but we were still soldiers with someone ordering us around every step of the way. The next few weeks were fast moving and chaotic. The debriefing was perfunctory at best; no one really seemed interested in hearing about a POW's life from the guys who lived it. The more rank the interviewer had the more certain he was he already knew all about it and there was nothing new we could tell him - even though he spent the entire war without coming within a hundred miles of the front. After a quick physical and a reintroduction to eating – nothing too exciting and not too much of it to start off - suddenly we were on a Gooney Bird bound for France and Camp Lucky Strike on the Normandy coast near Le Harve. Except for Lt Abele, who had been flown back to the States after his exchange, all the members of the crew of Lucifer II held a reunion at Camp Lucky Strike; all ten of us had survived and we were going home. There was some more waiting and another quick physical seemingly designed to make sure we were not bringing any dangerous bugs back to the States, but before long we sailed on a ship bound for New York, arriving 11 June 1945, sixty-five days after we marched away from our famous home away from home.

Editors note: The following excerpt is taken from the "H" section of the "Stalag XVII B US POW List" compiled by the son of S/Sgt.William J. Doubledee, USAAF, 8th AF, 351st BG, 511th BS. He has graciously published this list on his web site (http://www.stalag17b.com/index.htm) for public use. Uncle Mike's name appears in its place and the numbers and dates listed for him agree with those garnered from other sources, including his serial number indicating his Regular Army status. This is an exceptionally thorough and informative web site and the author deserves our thanks for making it available.

Name/ Stalag Bldg Captured (date)	Serial No/home.	type		Group		Missing Crew Rpt				
HECK CHARLES M 31B	35563427 IN	BMB	91	42-3506	3473	44	03		2	9
HEDRICK JOHN H 16B	13066366 VA	BMB	93	42-63964	2201	43	12		2	0
HEFFERNAN WILLIAM O 19A	15339050 OH	BMB	351	42-39905	1937	44	01		1	1
HEMMICK RALPH E 38A	16093121 WI	BMB	384	42-30037	x	43	06		2	6
HEMMINGER DONALD C 38A	39233691 CA	BMB	95	42-29689	4895	43	05		2	9
HENDERSON CHARLES H 39B	19059116 WA	BMB	92	42-29853	653	43	08		1	7
HENDERSON DAN S 37B	34125526 VA	BMB	44	42-7650	1376	43	11		1	3
HENDERSON ERNEST H 17B	38259045 LA	BMB	306	42-30173	822	43	10		1	4
HENDRIX HARLAND J 32A	19091460 CA	BMB	96	42-30665	2014	44	01		0	5
HENINGTON JESSE H 19B	6576453 CA	BMB	94	42-39767	1886	44	01		1	1
HENKEN NORMAN 32A	12154247 NY	BMB	384	42-31375	3820	44	04		1	1

HENLEY JAMES T 37B	38135316	TX	BMB	95	42-30211	4903	43	06	2	2
HENNEBERRY MICHAEL R 34A	R32405532	NY	BMB	384	42-29867	838	43	10	1	4
HENNESSEY JOSEPH T 35A	32470051	NY	BMB	379	42-37851	1719	43	12	2	0
HENNIS DAVID E 17B	15338242	WV	BMB	351	42-3152	876	43	10	0	9
HENRICKSON ROBERT M 17B	6912415	MO	BMB	384	42-29712	873	43	10	0	9
HENRY HARRY L 38B	33325811	PA	BMB	445	42-7554	15597	43	12	2	2
HENSON LLOYD E 15B	19004620	OR	BMB	17	?	x	43	01	1	4
HERALD CHARLIE F 37B	6984831	UNK	BMB	388	42-30234	3132	43	09	0	6
HERITAGE WILLIAM C 34B	15383125	IN	BMB	305	42-23550	921	43	10	1	4
HERMAN BANDY A 34B	34038340	NC	BMB	92	42-30231	844	43	10	1	4
HERMAN WILLIAM F 38A	20155756	RI	BMB	388	42-30234	3132	43	09	0	6
HERMANCE PAUL J 29A	12172216	NY	BMB	91	42-32072	4258	43	04	2	7
HERRERA PRESCILIANO S 32A	38120319	NM	BMB	384	42-31375	3820	44	04	1	1
HERRING GEORGE E 17A	19002595	CA	BMB	379	42-5820	1362	43	07	3	0
HERWIG RAYMOND L 18B	38092786	TX	BMB	319	?	x	42	12	0	4

A bunch of family members met me at the pier on New York City's west side. They seemed glad to see me. They had rented a couple of houses a short walk from the beach at Rockaway and we had a weekend-long party. I had been looking forward to a beer for a long time and when I finally tried one it tasted great but I couldn't finish it. By Sunday I was able to drink a whole one. I had felt pretty sick during the last few months in Stalag 17B and felt a lot worse during our forced march west but none of the military docs seemed to want to hear about it, either in France or back in the States. A few physicians later told me I should have been hospitalized at that point but I guess that fell though the cracks. I think there were just so many of us that the Brass didn't quite know what to do with us, which is understandable I suppose. There were suddenly millions of American citizen-soldiers clamoring to become civilians again. Almost 94,000 Americans were held as POWs in Europe during WWII and now that the European war was over somebody had to process us out. I was mustered out of the USAAF on 14 September 1945. I ventured forth to rebuild my life and see what else it had in store for me.

Part III

The Twilight Years

Chapter 13

Coming Home

After Uncle Mike's visit to us in Maine before he flew off to England in 1943, my next clear memory of him was the message from the War Department that he had been shot down and the clipping from the Yonkers' paper reporting him missing in action over Germany. About 20 months later my grandparents got the telegram from the Red Cross telling them that their son had turned up alive at the end of the war. The fact that he was alive at all, never mind coming home, was almost too much of a shock for them to handle. He had been "missing" for so long they had given up hope of ever seeing him again. This telegram was the first word they had received about him since the initial "missing in action" message.

Years later, while Uncle Mike and I toured the static displays of World War II aircraft at the Smithsonian Air and Space Museum in Washington, he spotted the very model parachute that had saved his neck and he opened up a little on his experiences in the war. He told me of his amazement on realizing it was really himself dangling from that chute. He told me about being taken in by a French family, and of being betrayed by them as he sat at their kitchen table munching on the apple they had offered. I was able to verify since then that his capture happened just the way he described it; the US Air Force Historical Studies Office sent me, along with a lot of other documents, the Missing Air Crew Report including the Casualty Questionnaire filed by crew member S/Sgt Al Wickline (page 125). Not that I doubted Uncle Mike's story, but Wickline's account supports not just my Uncle's credibility but his memory as well.

Like many POWs liberated from German camps at the end of the war, Uncle Mike came home to the US in sorry physical condition. Malnutrition, tuberculosis, and pancreatitis were the most serious of his many physical ailments; no one kept a scorecard on his psychic scars. His reception by his family didn't do much to help him put his life back together - there were no yellow ribbons waiting for him after the welcome home party. His brother Vinnie had slogged his way through the Italian campaign but then came home and went right back to work. His brother Joe went off to the Army too but developed a peptic ulcer which led to a disability retirement, so he too came home and went right back to work. Then Mike got home, and the family seemed to think that since the war was over and he was finally back it was time he got to work. In retrospect, it seems clear they had no conception of what POWs had faced and so they must be forgiven their indifference. To the returning POWs and other veterans of Viet Nam a few decades later, this may seem a familiar refrain.

So instead of staying home in Yonkers and starting life all over at 25, Uncle Mike decided to stay with the Army Air Corps - he thought they had more appreciation for the POWs who came back – and he reenlisted in 1946. Then began a decade interspersed with prolonged visits to various military hospitals as he was transferred around. He left most of one lung and another year of his life in Fitzsimmons Army Hospital in Denver. Finally, his physical problems forced him to seek a disability retirement from what was by then the US Air Force, and he began yet another phase of his life. There were rumors in the family back then that a lot of his problems came out of a bottle, but later, during one of his visits with us in Maryland - by which time he had long-since disavowed alcohol completely - he told me he had been pretty much a typical soldier who liked a few beers. It would not have taken much of a drinking problem to get him bounced from the peacetime Army or eliminated from gunnery school, or to prevent him from being assigned to a combat crew. So I have no reason to believe those rumors, and I have to conclude that his real problems began when his chute opened over France that spring afternoon in France in 1943.

This brings us to my uncle's "eclipse phase", from the late '50s to the early '80s, when his whereabouts were unknown to the rest of the clan and his death had again been assumed by most members of the family. As I later learned, he did a lot of moving around in those days,but I was never quite able to put the "where" with the "when". He became a real pro at Space-A travel, taking himself to parts of the world where his retirement pay would go the furthest. He spent a few years in Germany - of all places - and a few more in Mallorca; he often spoke of the warmth and economy of living on this, his favorite Mediterranean island. But he kept coming back to the US, favoring the Southwest for its climate. At the time of his retirement from the service his health wasn't much to brag about; it deteriorated steadily over the next 25 years. By the time of his first visit to us in 1983 he was well into his 60s and emphysema was slowing him seriously; it also added a strange little twist to his personality. He was probably what we used to call flippant in his best days. Later, with the chronic shortage of breath, his conversation seemed to consist mostly of phrases. Superimposed on an active sense of humor with a wry twist, this trait made it hard for many people to follow him - especially if they were poor listeners to begin with. Of course, I can't be sure this was the emphysema since his letters seemed to display a similar pattern, and so they were not too easy to follow either. But if you listened carefully, or read a little between the lines, you realized his humor was never far below the surface.

By the time of his visits to us, our slight-of-build Uncle Mike had a voracious appetite. He claimed his lack of pancreatic function kept him from digesting his food efficiently, and so it took a tremendous input to keep the fires burning. I'm not sure about the reason, but he ate more than any of our growing kids ever did. He seemed to do okay on four standard-size meals per day - provided there was plenty to snack on in between.

My wife Pat and Uncle Mike used to have a lot of conversations during his visits. Pat recalls one particular day while they were sitting in the kitchen over a cup of coffee and Uncle Mike asked her about her family. Along with the usual family history, she got around to telling him that she had relatives in the Revolutionary War, the Civil War, and the Spanish American War and went on to tell him the story of her father in World War I and her brothers in WW II and Korea.

As usual, Uncle Mike was interested in hearing about any relatives who served in the military, and he seemed especially impressed to learn Pat's dad, Francis J Roderer, served as a Lieutenant in the 604th Engineer Regiment as part of the 1st Infantry Division - the famous "Big Red One" - in France from 1917 until Armistice Day 1918. He had joined the Army in 1913; was selected for Officers Training School (OCS); was commissioned as a Lieutenant; and served in the Mexican Punitive Expedition in pursuit of Pancho Villa from 1916 until the US entered the war in 1917.

Uncle Mike seemed very familiar with the history of WW I including the names of all the battles and he wondered if Pat knew which battles her father fought in in Europe so she told him the ones her father had mentioned: Cantigny; Ypres; Argonne Forest; and Messines. He seemed to get a real kick out of hearing these stories and mentioned he wished he had met Pat's father. Pat felt that this conversation did a lot to cement their relationship and she thought Uncle Mike liked his nephew's wife much better after that.

Lt Francis J Roderer

France, 1918

Strangely enough, we soon learned that Uncle Mike and our son Mike shared a remarkable talent for mimicry; either would have been a suitable replacement for Mel Blanc or Jim Backus. We had thought our son acquired this from his love of the Saturday morning cartoons as he was growing up, but maybe there is a Henneberry gene for this from way back there somewhere. Uncle Mike had apparently used this talent both as a POW and on Armed Forces Radio at some point during his California phase; it seems he had a disc jockey show specializing in music from the Big Band era interspersed with his own special brand of patter in the voices of a handful of characters. On one of his trips east in the 80s he brought us an old reel-to-reel tape of one of his shows; he was thoroughly familiar with the music and was a very funny man in his prime. By the time I grew to know him later in our lives his health was slowing him greatly, but I got the impression that he was a funny guy who had always wanted to be Henny Youngman when he grew up. Unfortunately, he grew up too suddenly and too soon.

Life was not all laughs when Uncle Mike came to visit. Once, shortly after he arrived, my wife and I had to be in Colorado for a week - leaving Mike alone with our teen-aged son Rich. As fate would have it, Mike became ill with what seemed to be a bad cold; he took to his bed and relied on Rich for his sustenance. Rich still tells of the cries for "JUICE! JUICE!" echoing from Uncle Mike's room at all hours of the day and night. Despite

Rich's ministrations, Mike's condition worsened and Rich took him off to the National Naval Medical Center in Bethesda, Maryland, our family's usual source of medical care. Mike was sick enough to be admitted and Rich left him settled comfortably on the third floor. After school the next day Rich went straight to the Medical Center to see how his uncle was doing, but was surprised to find Mike's bed empty. In response to Rich's inquiry, a young Navy nurse casually replied "Oh, he's gone". Rich took the worst possible meaning from this comment and was stricken with a major case of distress consisting of equal parts grief for his uncle and fear of what his father would do to him for letting Uncle Mike die on his watch. Recognizing Rich's reaction, the nurse quickly added "I mean we moved him to room 309". Mike must have been confused by the emotional nature of their reunion moments later. For his part, Rich was greatly relieved to be off the hook and was even happier a few days later to bring Mike home again before we returned from our trip.

We learned that Uncle Mike's illness was due to an overdose of theophylline, a drug used for many years for the treatment of breathlessness. It had been prescribed for him for his COPD. Too low a dose does not sufficiently help breathing while too high a dose causes illness. Uncle Mike realized later that he had increased the dose driving over the Rockies and not decreased it enough afterwards. There is an excellent chance Uncle Mike's lung problems stemmed from the smoking habit he had begun to cultivate at age 12. In those days most America men and a lot of American women had taken up the habit. I doubt if there were any POWs who didn't smoke. The Red Cross routinely included cigarettes in its Care Packages. But that was before the US Surgeon General warned the public of the hazards of smoking. Of course long before that alert every smoker must have realized there was a relationship between his smoking and his breathlessness, but that was not on the list of things POWs had to worry about.

While there was certainly affection between Rich and Uncle Mike it wasn't always smooth sailing. Mike could be cranky and demanding, especially when he was tired, and Rich was a teen-ager with a teen-ager's patience level. I never saw a serious conflagration but sparks flew now and then. During the summer of 1983 Uncle Mike wanted to drive from our home in Maryland to visit our son Mike who by then was in Navy Divers School in Panama City, Florida. Not looking forward to another long drive alone, he convinced Rich to go along with him. I think they were gone about two weeks and all I know is they survived but I got the impression from Rich that he wouldn't be volunteering to do that again.

As if the meeting of the two Michaels in Hawaii were not enough of a coincidence, I always felt that there was an added element of serendipity in this story because of subsequent events as have been described here. Lately, it has become stylish for the more religious or superstitious among us to attribute such events to supernatural intervention and for the more "objective analysts" to brush aside the most unlikely of coincidences, characterizing them as the inevitable consequences of the laws of chance. Heaven forbid we should succumb to our too-human tendency to attach any significance to even the most far-fetched happenings. One current popular psychology concept is that we are often overly impressed by coincidental occurrences within our own families because we like to think we are special. Maybe so, but read on.

Uncle Mike had already begun searching for his roots, and his chance encounter with his namesake was a major - if totally unanticipated - step in that direction. His next step was to embark on his first trip to Ireland to search out the village his father had left many years before. Some brilliant detective work and more than a grain of perseverance on his part led him to the family farm, still active but no longer in Henneberry hands. In visiting St. Declan's parish church in the village of Ardmore, County Waterford where his father was born, he ran into another dead end. It seems a fire some years earlier had destroyed the parish archives, the usual depository of birth certificates and marriage license records. However, the old Irish priest remembered that there had been Henneberrys in Ardmore until the last one died, probably in the early 1960s, and that for several years before that a young cousin came from Wales to spend each summer on the family farm up until the time he entered the seminary at Manooth. As he told me the story later, a simple phone call to Ireland's National Seminary provided the information he needed; only one seminarian named Henneberry had ever finished there and after his ordination he returned to his native Wales where he was serving as pastor of the Roman Catholic parish in Cardiff. Soon Mike made his way to Rosslare and the ferry to Fishguard across the Irish Sea, and traveled by bus across the width of Wales where he found the address of the Catholic Church in the phone book and was soon knocking on the door of the rectory.

This was cold-calling taken to the extreme and I imagine it took Uncle Mike a few minutes to tell his story to a very surprised priest. And so Father Colin Henneberry, the grandson of my grandfather's brother, entered our lives. His existence was not known to anyone in the American side of the family before Uncle Mike's discovery. I am sure my grandfather knew of Colin, but Pop had passed away more than twenty years earlier. When I was a boy, Pop had orchestrated a pen-pal relationship between me and another cousin in Wales, Barney Henneberry, grandson of another of my grandfather's brothers. Barney and I had exchanged letters for several years but lost touch with each other as the high school years consumed our time and attention. I remembered that Barney's father had been involved in the aviation industry and I was, as a pilot myself, quite pleased to learn later through Colin that Barney was a pilot flying the big iron for British Airways.

Before my wife Pat and I ever met Colin we learned about him from Uncle Mike and on a subsequent trip to Ireland we decided to travel to Wales on our way to London. On the spur of the moment, we realized it wouldn't be much out of our way to visit Cardiff and decided to surprise Colin with a visit. Our plan backfired when we arrived at his rectory only to find he was on a golfing holiday in the Ireland we had just left. So the first time we met Father Henneberry was when we met his plane arriving at Dulles airport; he was recognizable from the family resemblance. Colin spent a pleasant month with us at our home in Maryland that year and learned two important lessons about America: he found a baseball game in Baltimore to be baffling but he found he really liked Miller Lite Beer. He also liked taking long walks through the woods with our two German Shepherds and lamented the fact that he had been forced to leave his dog at home. He was an avid golfer and I'm sure he was sorry to hear there were no golfers in the family. On one occasion I drove Colin to a public course not far from home but, due to two deteriorated hip joints awaiting replacement, I was unable to go around the course with him. I was forced to wait in the 19th hole where I ran into a fellow I knew at work before he retired; Colin drove me home on that occasion - on the wrong side of the road for much of the way . I enjoyed Colin's visit and between us we filled in a lot of blanks on the family tree - but that is another story. We were in the process of planning Colin's second trip to visit us a few years later when we had the shocking news that he had died of a sudden heart attack on the golf course, playing the game he loved. He was 56 years old.

So Uncle Mike's travel adventures had turned up yet another relative. His wanderlust didn't fade as he moved into his late 60s, but it was defeated by advancing years and ill health. Although he continued to make plans, he had taken his last Space-A trip.

Father Colin Henneberry relaxes in Maryland with his friends Kieran (l) and Shandy (r).

Chapter 14

Taps

On Thanksgiving of 1988, I mailed off my regular fall letter to Uncle Mike at his California apartment. By a few weeks before Christmas I realized I hadn't received the usual reply and resolved to call him Christmas Eve. But a day or so later I got a call from him and it was obvious from his voice that his health was failing; he said he'd be checking into the local military hospital and gave me the phone numbers of two friends so I could stay in touch. He brushed it off as just some abdominal pain that wouldn't quit, but I could not help but wonder what was really going on.

Several years earlier Uncle Mike had requested and received permission to be buried in Arlington National Cemetery and asked me to see to the arrangements when the time came. Then, two days before Christmas he called again - excited over a letter he had just received with his acceptance into the Soldier's and

Airmen's Home in Washington, a first-class operation maintained by the US government for the last years of our otherwise homeless distinguished veterans including POWs. It is quite difficult to gain admission to the Home due to insufficient space. It can accommodate only a small fraction of those who earned the right to live out their lives in such a place - yet another example of the promises the world's richest country made to its soldiers and later broke. It is still at it with its failure to provide adequate care for its damaged veterans returning from our perpetual and seemingly futile wars. Mike had to be persistent to gain acceptance to the Soldiers's and Airman's Home; he had first applied several years earlier but had heard nothing until he had the bright idea of involving his congressman and reminding everyone of his POW status.

I began to realize that Uncle Mike's medical problems were more serious than he had let on when he told me the Air Force would Air-Evac him from California to Washington DC within the next few days. I visited him at the Health Care Center at the Soldier's home when he arrived the last Friday in December of '88. It was obvious he had lost some weight, seemed a little confused, and was having some pain. But he seemed to be in pretty good spirits and we kidded a little before I left.

New Year's Day we had a pretty good snowstorm – the kind that shuts DC down for several days - and we were forced to postpone our next visit until Monday. When we arrived at the Soldier's Home we learned Mike had been transferred the day before to the VA Hospital a few blocks away. Somebody had forgotten to notify the next of kin - me. By the time we tracked him down at the VA hospital that afternoon he was in intensive care, the abdominal pain had worsened sharply, and he was obviously weaker. By Wednesday, his kidney and liver functions had begun to fail and it was agreed that it was imperative to open the abdominal cavity; the best guess - or at least what I was told - was that an inflamed gallbladder might have kicked off his snowballing problems. What they found was advanced metastatic cancer, previously undiagnosed. A very sensitive young surgeon told me gently that Uncle Mike's days were numbered. Mercifully, my Uncle's heart stopped two days later without his ever regaining consciousness. He died without knowing he had a terminal illness.

On 11 January 1989, fifty-two years and a lot of miles after he enlisted in the Army at age seventeen, and 24 days shy of his 70th birthday, SSgt Michael R Henneberry, USAF (Ret) was buried at Arlington National Cemetery with military honors – including the Seven-Gun Salute and, of course, Taps - guaranteed not to leave a dry eye in the house. When it comes to burials, nobody does it better than the US Army folks at Arlington. Old Mike would have loved it.

Thus, by way of the final improbable event in a chain of improbable events that had started 6,000 miles away in Pearl Harbor with a highly improbable encounter, Uncle Mike managed to be with the only family he had at the end. The Old Soldier had come home to die.

The End

Michael R Henneberry (1920-1989)

Member, Greatest Generation

Further Reading

The Mighty Eighth Air Force
A History of the US 8th Army Air Force
Roger A Freeman, 1970
Doubleday and Company, New York

American Prisoners of War in Germany
Chapter: Stalag 17 B, 1 November 1945
Military Intelligence Service
War Department
Washington DC

Toscanini's Fumble: Wapniarka
Harold L Klawans, MD
ISBN 0-553-34662-8
Bantam Books, 1989

Jump, Damn It, Jump
Edward F Logan, Jr
ISBN-13: 978-0-7864-2572-3
McFarland & Co, NC 2006

World War Two:
from a Waist Gunner's View of Stalag 17
S/Sgt Luther Irwin Kelly, 2008
ISBN-13: 978-1-4363-2505-9

Black Thursday [Illustrated Edition]
by Martin Caidin
Kindle Edition, 2015, Amazon.com

My father in World War II
Robert H Penoyer
www.bobpenoyer.com/DAD6b.pdf

Stalag 17 B
Eric Ethier
http://www.americainwwii.com/articles/stalag-17-b/

Stalag 17B web page
http://www.stalag17b.com/history.html

Schweinfurt II web page
http://www.historynet.com/world-war-ii-eighth-air-force-raid-on-schweinfurt.htm

Aerial Gunners Schools web page
GJJM http://www.zenoswarbirdvideos.com/WW2GunnerySchool.html

And many other easily located, dedicated web sites containing extraordinary quantities of high-quality information.

About the Author:

After growing up in the Berkshires of Western Massachusetts and paying his dues in college; the Air Force; graduate school; and post-doctoral studies, the author settled into a research career in biomedicine as a member of the United States Public Health Service (our little-known seventh Uniformed Service). A self-described compulsive writer, he soon began to make time for churning out a string of essays and short stories when he wasn't writing scientific papers. His stories reflect his interests in family life and his involvements in flying, skiing and restoring old sports cars. In this book, 20 years in the making, he tells the story of his Uncle Mike's life as a soldier, an airman, and a prisoner-of war - a man who was separated from his entire family for more than 25 years until rediscovered by the author's son in Pearl Harbor in 1983 in a remarkable coincidence. Now retired, the author lives in Viera, Florida with his wife Pat and their German Shepherd. They spend their summers in the Berkshires and enjoy frequent visits with their four children and six grandchildren.

Made in the USA
Charleston, SC
02 November 2015